How the spirit of surfing showed me the way
to the kind of success that makes life worth living.

CHRISTOPHER
BROWN

First published in 2019 by Taco Stand Pty Limited.

Copyright © Christopher Brown 2019.
All rights reserved.

FROTH AND HUSTLE
www.frothandhustle.com

All illustrations by Monez Gusmang. Copyright © Monez 2019.
www.monez.net

First edition
This AU English print edition first published in 2019.
ISBN: 978-0-6485433-1-2 Paperback
ISBN: 978-0-6485433-0-5 Ebook
ISBN: 978-0-6485433-2-9 Kindle

 A catalogue record for this book is available from the National Library of Australia

For Mum & Dad.

*When you reach the peak and just want to jump off...*

My final six months of working in the corporate world, had been a roller coaster of escalating highs and stomach wrenching lows.

I thought I'd reached the pinnacle of my career. I had finally achieved the success I always dreamed of. But on one pivotal night, when I found myself sleeping on the bathroom floor, I had a life-altering realisation.

It was all a load of crap. My role as Director of this multi-national company, was literally ending in a load of crap...

A hotel medic burst into the room shouting loudly on his two-way, "The guest is conscious and breathing, I repeat, the guest is conscious and breathing".

The tiny hotel room was filled with a smell beyond description. And in typical Las Vegas style, there were no windows for respite. The medic brought with him a large blue duffel bag; a white cross emblazoned on the side. I was saved. After assuring him I was in fact alive, I pleaded with him to give me something to stop the vomiting.

"Sir, I cannot do that." His tone was unsympathetic.

"Then what the fuck is in that bag?" I replied. I got it now, he wasn't there to help. He was there to check I wasn't dead. The medic left the room as ceremoniously as he'd arrived, the door slamming me tightly inside what had started to feel like a desolate corner of hell.

I had called the concierge earlier in the night begging for an aspirin or paracetamol, anything to help stop the vomiting. They wouldn't give me a thing.

Instead, I lay on the floor in absolute agony. My guts contorting and turning inside my body. Every joint ached. My head pounded. And my temperature fluctuated between fire and ice.

As the early morning light peeked through the heavy curtains, a sense of relief began to sweep over me. I made it through to the other side. But I almost wished I hadn't. The lobster we'd been served for dinner had really done a number on me. It was the last thing left on my plate and just like when I was a kid, I'd eaten around it to save the 'best' for last.

Toward the end of dinner service, the waiter came to take the uneaten poison away and I'd almost let him. Instead, I uttered the fatal words, "Sorry, I'm not finished yet." In hindsight, I should have trusted the universe, the waiter or at the very least my nose.

You should always trust your nose.

The dinner had been part of a welcoming event for our business partners, hosted by our company's new owners. I'd flown halfway around the world for this occasion, the importance of which was not lost on me. The evening had gone extremely well. Australia was a place they didn't have to worry about, something I was extremely proud of. We ran a tight ship and had worked hard to become one of the most profitable regions in the world.

From swimming in praise to exploding from both ends, I could hardly believe the night had happened. Aside from meeting my new manager, I was scheduled to sit down with our major retailer and partner distributor the very next day. But due to the 'wholesome' lobster, I was doomed to miss it. It would take a miracle for me to make it out of the room. I knew the shit would hit the fan and there was nothing I could do. It took every cell in my body to summon the energy to call the boss, contact the distributor to apologise and lay down on the bed, hoping for a sudden recovery. But it never came. I missed the meeting and my scheduled flight home.

Much later that day, with a pounding headache and several kilos lighter, I gathered my belongings and left for the airport, completely unaware of the other shit-storm, which started brewing in my absence.

When I finally arrived back in Australia, my withered stomach lurched into my throat as I read through the emails telling me what happened in the meeting I'd missed. I was overwhelmed with horror; I couldn't believe it. My character, my ability, my passion even, were being brought in to question.

Our 'partner' distributor had used my absence from the meeting to launch a campaign to undermine me and my support colleague in an attempt to gain full control of the brand in Australia. If successful, it would remove any policing and influence in the brand's best interest. It would mean they could do as they pleased with the business we'd proudly worked so hard to build. The reasoning used to support their takeover was fictional beyond belief and couldn't have been further from the truth. The betrayal brought with it a sickening lesson.

I'd sampled a taste of a very ugly side of business. It was confronting and horrible.

All of the hard work, patience and most disappointingly, the trust we had established, all pissed away. And why? It was stupid. However, for me this wouldn't be the last time, there was more, much more to come.

The dream career, the dream company, everything I'd worked the last twenty years for, was turning out to be a bloody nightmare. And it was all completely unexpected.

How and where did it all go so horribly wrong?

*Introduction*

My goal is simple. To live an authentic life, true to what I feel, without boundaries. I want to be free to explore, to go where the wind blows and where my heart leads me.

This is both far harder and much easier than it sounds. It's only by looking back at my life, I can see and appreciate just how all of my experiences and decisions shaped me and my desires. And despite times of frustration and desperation, just how fortunate I have actually been.

In the end, what it took was a change in perspective and an open, flexible mind to find success in the two most significant parts of my life - surfing and business. The success I craved was simple: the freedom to surf whenever I want and a sustainable business that would allow me to do this. These two things became my ultimate pursuit, they became my whole life, and the approach I took, became what I call - Froth & Hustle.

I don't believe in fate, destiny or coincidence. I believe in myself, my instincts and my choices.

Fear and comfort were the self-imposed shackles that inhibited my ability for growth. They influenced all the decisions I'd made, the minor risks I'd taken, successes I celebrated and all the failures I endured. I desired freedom but lacked the courage to take the big leaps. But by changing my perspective and re-writing my own tired stories, I learned to trust in myself and my instincts. Curiosity led me to discovery.

We have the means to challenge everything around us, but we also need to challenge ourselves. We get just one life to do so. If we embrace the randomness that's always-present in life, we can let go of the limiting expectations that hold us back.

Mastering Froth & Hustle, through both the good and the tough times, transformed my life. I've created my own nirvana and carved out my own professional path by adopting a different life philosophy. A philosophy governed by freedom and choice.

This is the story of how I scaled the heights of my corporate career only to find myself in the lows of unemployment, and how the regular practise of surfing helped me start again from the bottom, to build my own business with the freedom to work from anywhere in the world.

Part memoir and part personal philosophy, I hope you find something inside. Perhaps a different way of seeing the future.

As Bill Murray said, "This is not a dress rehearsal; this is your life."

*A little bit about me*

As early as I can remember, I'd always done things my own way. I preferred to discover the answers for myself, connecting to the world through the people I met and the relationships I built. While my school grades might have been average, I developed faster in other ways. I held an ever-shifting, independently curious view of the world, which I happily challenged and tested at every opportunity.

As a kid, I was self-confident and precocious. But I absorbed everything. I remember hearing the adults around me often complain about their work and complain about life. This open dissatisfaction ingrained in me the belief that when we got older, we don't have a choice. Life was somehow predetermined; we were to play the hands we're dealt and just make do. It sounded like such a gloomy world, where we are the sum of our place, our family, our education, our status and our wealth. None of it made sense to me then, but given the pure frustration people displayed openly for the life they themselves created, what else was I to believe?

When I did learn we have a choice, nothing is predetermined and we are what we create, it came as an incredible relief and a critical turning point.

As I got older, I became more comfortable challenging the standard formula than trying to fit in. I enjoyed making fun and light of the seriousness I often found myself surrounded by. From the moment I could work, I made a promise to myself to never allow my job to dominate my world or dictate who I would become. This part was up to me. I was determined not to be another despondent soul.

In revolt I devised a plan, to always treat life like an adventure. To not be rigid or struggle to fit-in, but instead be flexible and adaptable in the way I approached things. I would always look forward, trust in myself and my own abilities. I believed if I followed my instincts the jigsaw would eventually fall into place. But like many maturing adults making decisions about their future, I found the illusion and comfort of routine alluring. Until I was forced to discover the delights of discomfort.

I experimented with many roles during my early working-life. But I found myself drawn to those with greater independence, creativity and autonomy, shaping and sharpening my craft, before eventually connecting the dots that would lead me to a career. I found something that existed outside the norm, forged by my own experiences, failures and successes.

I was always too selfish and curious to settle for the safety found in the status quo. I craved something unique and of my own creation. But I went through a great deal before I could recognise my natural strengths and the true opportunities in front of me. I had to embrace all my natural weaknesses and view the obstacles and challenges as necessary pathways toward growth.

I'd once fantasised about making a living doing what I loved. Now I can't imagine anything else, as today, I do just that. The chances I took and changes I made are responsible for me turning my work into my art, my absolute passion, which thrives in an unrestricted and limitless environment. I never understood or appreciated what true wealth or real freedom was, not until I created my own version of it.

In 2016, my wife and I decided to live the life we always wanted. We threw away all preconceptions and doubt to embrace the unknown. To discover for ourselves what was really possible. Today we don't fit in, instead we live and work in an alternative way. Our goal is to continue exploring the world, building our companies, surfing in beautiful and remote locations and being free.

Like everyone, I am the result of millions of decisions, experiences and influences. I am a product of my environment and mind. To help me understand what set me on my chosen path, I had to go back to my earliest and most influential memories. Doing so became a cathartic process, as I clearly connected my passions and desires from my experiences as a kid, through to the career and life choices that brought me to where I am today.

During my childhood, my father was a stern man, understandably as his father was also stern. He grew up on the cane fields of northern Queensland, until he relocated to Sydney where he pursued self-employment. He worked very long hours, well into most nights. Self-motivated, he built himself a well-deserved reputation as an expert, having mastered antique clock and watch repairs.

Dad always was and still is, very good with people. He has a particular way about him, like a contagious lightness and sense of humour he could apply to almost anything or anyone. Except when us kids got in trouble.

I've come to appreciate later in life, just how much the old man did for Mum and us kids. His hard exterior surrounded an enormous heart and he always remained sympathetic and caring. This was especially clear during my mother's final years before she passed away from Alzheimer's Dementia in late 2014.

My mother immigrated from England to Australia in her teens. She was a gentle and caring woman, who always made me feel special and unique. We were very close. Mum was compassionate, as my father says she didn't have a single bad bone in her body. She encouraged and inspired me in so many ways. She loved music and would fill the house with Simon & Garfunkel, Neil Diamond and Bob Dylan. She rarely got angry, even when I tested the boundaries in my teens and even more so into my twenties. I was one of four kids and we were her world. I miss her dearly.

Except for Mum, we were not the sort of family to say "I love you" very often. We showed our love for each other in different ways. We were mostly left to our own devices and given the space to learn our way through the world, with some of us navigating through rougher patches. We were taught to think for ourselves and given the freedom to do what we wanted. It took me a long time to appreciate just how fortunate we were to be brought up in this way. We learned from our own mistakes and were taught to deal with the consequences independently.

The first two years of my life were spent on Sydney's Northern Beaches, before we moved to Canberra where Dad built his watchmaking business. I stayed in Canberra for eighteen years, at times it was a beautiful city, particularly in the changing seasons, but for an adventurous soul it can be an extremely boring town. The advantages of sporting culture, skate-parks and one of Australia's coolest music stores, Impact Records, lost their appeal when I reached my twenties and decided it was time to pursue my own path away from the familiarity of home.

Today, as I sit out in the ocean, hands moving slowly through the crystal-clear water, sun shining warmly on my back, reality hits me.

I live here. I really live here.

In the distance, palm trees sway gently, marking the shoreline of my favourite beach. I'm surrounded only by a deep and calming silence. It's just me, my surfboard and my passing thoughts. This island paradise is where I now live.

Bali holds a special place in my heart, it's my adopted spiritual home. An escape for the last twelve years, it was the only place where I felt I could centre myself, recharge and breathe. The familiar scent of frangipanis and incense as I stepped off the plane is tattooed firmly on my brain, along with a sense of absolute freedom. My twice-yearly surf trips washed away any stress or anxieties from the hectic Sydney lifestyle I had been living. It would always bring me back to myself, even if only temporarily.

Now life had taken a turn and I'd landed here for an unknown period of time, surrounded by some of the world's best surf. Gone were the days of too short visits to paradise. In the rich Balinese culture, it often feels there is an endless string of magical places just waiting to be explored.

But I had to take numerous risks and a giant leap of faith to get here. The reason I'm now achieving a definition of success I'd only before dreamt of was not just because of who I was as a person. The reason I was able to live in a country other people holiday to, was because once upon a time I hit the heights of my career only to lose it all through some of the hardest lessons. Life changing failures forced me into a process of re-evaluation and redefining what I believed. It led me to challenge myself and ultimately, to change my perspective and mindset.

Whenever I hit the majestic waves, I suspected there was a deeper more meaningful connection happening. And now as I sit in the warm clear water, coral reef below me, I can see this is just the start of it. Taking the chance to move to Bali might have marked the end of my official corporate Sydney lifestyle, but it was just the beginning of the rest of my journey.

# PART ONE
# HUSTLE

Hustle:
"to work with speed and vigour"
"to make things happen"

In 2010, I was living the 'schmick' corporate life. I achieved everything I thought would make me incredibly happy. I was driving a sporty car, taking regular trips overseas, dressed in designer suits, had cash in the bank and was surfing every morning. Life couldn't get better. Or so I thought.

I was breaking new ground and winning awards with the international company I worked for. My work, my achievements and my way of doing things were being recognised and respected all the way to the top. I was in control of a key part of the business, which was thriving. I had the autonomy and freedom to steer it where I wanted and had plenty of support from the folks in charge to make it happen.

My relationship with my manager was great, we laughed as hard as we worked. Our achievements took us around the globe to exotic locations such as Hawaii and the Caribbean.

All the long hours and dedication to my work was worth it. I felt success, at last. But it wasn't through the route of an MBA, nor was my education at an expensive business school. All of the skills I'd developed that made me successful, were gained from a combination of life lessons, learning how to make things work and a pure ambition to create more.

Hustle didn't start for me when I got my first sales job or role in a corporate business. My Hustle began when I was very young. It came about because I was left to my own defences. I had to take responsibility for myself.

It wasn't just the 'hard' skills of number crunching, proposals and business plans that helped me reach my career successes. It was the 'soft' skills I was compelled to learn in my childhood and teenage years - confidence, relationship building, resilience - the ones you don't learn at business school, which set me on a path toward a career I loved. And these were the critical skills I needed to call on when things went in a direction I never could have planned for. It was these skills that got me through the tough times when I thought I was going to lose everything.

These 'soft' skills - or more honestly, 'life' skills, are essential for achieving long-term success and satisfaction in your career. They are the learned skills you can develop with focus, introspection and trial and error at any age.

Hustle is NOT about knowing how to manipulate people to achieve your own goals.

Hustle is knowing how to shape and mould yourself, how to work to your highest level and how to make things happen, through sheer effort, will and belief in yourself.

# CHAPTER ONE
*Natural confidence is something you learn*

They say, "you're either born with it or you're not". But contrary to common belief, confidence is not something that comes in your gene-pool, it's a learned behaviour and learned way of thinking.

Lucky for me, I lived in the perfect environment to build confidence from an early age. With three much older siblings in the house, I had little choice but to be outspoken and independent. It proved extremely helpful to get what I wanted in life.

I spent most of my youth desperately seeking my older brothers' approval. The years between us created a disconnection I endlessly tried to connect. I looked up to them. Everything they did was cool. But all attempts I made to get their attention only seemed to broaden the gap. I hated being the youngest and just wanted to be older, like them. But I later learned the value of what this brought out in me.

I was much closer to my sister than my brothers. Some of my earliest memories are of me perched on her hip, as she'd take me everywhere. I always felt more comfortable with her, probably because I could act my own age. I didn't feel I had to change myself or be someone I wasn't. We spent a lot of time together and as I got older, I would think of her boyfriends as my new brothers.

Having older siblings forced me to try harder and taught me the value of being loved for who I was. This environment heavily influenced my natural confidence and exposed me to older behaviours and interests, which often got me into trouble at school.

As a kid I talked a lot to anyone who'd listen, so I found it very easy to make friends. I liked to be liked and hated to be disliked, misunderstood or ignored. I never really felt comfortable asking my brothers or sister for advice. It seemed easier to make a mistake and learn from it, than face the embarrassment. This turned out to be a blessing in disguise as my curiosity and confidence grew. Although it was hard at times, I realised if I was to make my way through life, I had to just try things and fail.

I knew I was good at some things and not so good at others. I accepted that 'Top of the Class' wasn't something I was cut out for. I dreaded parent and teacher evenings. Year after year, teachers would repeat the same assessment, "full of potential, but too easily distracted". And year after year, despite my efforts, little would change. It's not like I didn't try, I was just more interested in other things, the things I discovered by myself.

It didn't matter how random or strange, if something caught my attention, I had to know everything about it. From sports to drawing pictures of shark-attacks, I would spend my free time passionately absorbed, until I had mastered it. If I found it interesting, I invested energy in it like I was investing in myself. I invested this same energy socially too.

I mostly learned about the world through the people I would meet and the relationships I developed outside of my family. I wanted to see the world through other people's eyes. This gave me a sense of belonging to something bigger, of being a part of not just a family, but of the wider landscape of what it meant to be alive. Understanding this was important to me, my surroundings gave me a sense of self and a place where I could fit in. I didn't like feeling lost or confused, so I questioned everything around me, all the time listening, absorbing, building a picture of where I belonged.

A huge part of finding my way was my unquenchable desire to try anything, at least once. I prided myself on being the first to put my hand up for any new challenge, whether it was sports, school plays, anything. By putting myself out there I developed a willingness to do the things others wouldn't.

My mother's encouragement reinforced my confidence and enabled me to feel I was on the right track, even when I challenged myself and made mistakes. Confidence began to come naturally for me, it wasn't a conscious choice, it was simply the way I'd learned to be. This helped me greatly through life and soon my confidence, even when facing the unknown, became the basis of my ability to connect with people.

## CHAPTER TWO

*Hustle is about relationships first*

When you are completely present with the person you're talking to, it enables you to connect on a level people respond to and it cuts through all the bullshit and distractions. This requires you to not think about your own agenda, but to listen and hear more than just the words coming out of a person's mouth. In business this improves your chances of getting what you want - by knowing exactly what it is the other person needs.

A critical component of communication is understanding how we make someone feel. Paying attention to the impact you have on others, guides you on what to say next and it allows you to communicate directly to an individual, tapping into their current state of mind. This was one of the things I learnt at a young age. Sparked by a desire to understand more about people, I sought opportunities to connect with strangers and make new friends.

My first memory of learning the importance of how we make people feel was when I was six. I was at the park with my brother and his friend. They spotted some girls they wanted to talk to but as awkward pre-teens, they didn't have the courage to approach them. My brother asked me to break the ice and at age six, I didn't get what the big deal was. I loved talking with and meeting new people, so had no hesitation walking straight up to them. That afternoon, I spent more time talking to the girls than hanging out with my brother.

It wasn't until we were about to leave, one of the girls turned to me and commented, "When you get older, you gonna make some lucky girl very happy." This made me feel special in some way. Even if I didn't understand what it really meant, it didn't matter because I distinctly remember how the words made me feel. The time I'd spent asking questions and listening must have had an impact on them and it certainly had a positive impact on me.

I always found it easy and fun to relate to other people. And by doing it often I discovered my own style of communication. Deep down I think we all prefer to smile and have a laugh, so I found a light and playful approach was always better received. As I got older, I realised how effective this was at removing barriers and connecting with others.

During my primary school years, I spent hours at our local 'Adventure Playground' - called 'Adventure' because it had giant swings, concrete half-pipe, long slippery dips, flying foxes and a 'Tarzan rope'. The Tarzan rope was an infamous rite of passage for local kids. I wanted to ride it so bad, but every time I'd go to the playground, it would be swarmed by a group of tough local kids. Closer to my brother's age, they were the kind of kids who were into graffiti and wore black jeans with 'flannies' (standard issue for local goons in the eighties). Because of them, most kids avoided the Tarzan rope altogether, but I would watch them launching from the highest row of seats, yahooing each other as they'd take it in turns. I refused to accept I couldn't have a go too.

I was just a skinny little runt back then, but I knew if I wanted to ride the Tarzan rope, I'd have to win the tough kids over. The only things I had going for me were I could talk to anyone and I was used to people their age. I imagined if I were them, what would I like and what would I not. They could've just told me to piss off, like they did everyone else and I would have. But they didn't. After a few minutes, I had my first go on the rope.

As I worked my way into their group, I actually started to enjoy their company. Soon they were treating me like one of their own. My experience with these kids taught me some fundamental lessons. Firstly, about people's perception of others and how we need to challenge those perceptions to create our own. People judge far too quickly, me included. Once I broke through their hard exterior, these kids were fine, they were like anyone else. In some ways even friendlier. Secondly, developing friendships takes effort and practice. You need to be able to fit in a group dynamic and also connect with people individually.

If I'd taken this group of kids at face value, I never would have gotten what I wanted. If we're quick to judge or make up our mind about a situation, person or potential opportunity without all the information or without diving in to test the water, then we don't get a chance to discover the warm undercurrent that exists below a cold or tough surface. Many business relationships fail or fall short simply for this one reason. Never let first impressions prevent you from finding out what is possible.

By the time I hit the final years of high school, I was part of a large diverse group of close friends. We were a cumulation of sporto's, hoodlums, skaters and artistic types, brought together by our love of wild parties.

Most weekends, we'd converge at someone's house, unbeknownst to their parents. We'd play music, drink too much and a handful of us would stay up into the early morning to watch 'Rage' countdown the top video hits. It was around this time I discovered Pink Floyd and art-house films, which had a big influence as we tried to out-cool each other with our alternative tastes.

During these years, I seemed to bounce from feeling like I was on top of the world to being lost in a world of confusion. But everyone else seemed to be in the same state of teenage angst, so I considered it part of life. A not so fun part. Through it all however, we had each other, there was always someone around to bounce off. It gave us a chance to meet new people, make mistakes, find ourselves and grow up in one giant mess together.

It was in this group where I met Tobey. We were very similar in the things we liked and different in our own way from the rest of our friends. Both of us struggled with grades but we excelled in acting out. We partied, drank his father's home-brew and skate-boarded our way through high school together. By the end, we were inseparable best mates.

Most of what we got up to was harmless fun. We'd walk the streets after a few too many home-brews and wake up in the morning to find his tennis court littered with trophies from our adventures.

In our final year of school however, Tobey suddenly died from a tragic random accident. The impact this had on me was something I carried for a very long time. For me, Tobey was one of a kind, I'd never before connected with a mate the way I had with him. It was like we could read each other's thoughts as we encouraged the best (and worst) in each other.

I don't remember my family saying much to me about Tobey's death, we just weren't the sort of family who shared feelings. However, I do remember my mum trying very hard to console me as we cried together. But still, the loss of my best mate was not something anyone could understand, it was something I'd have to navigate on my own.

I have thought about Tobey many times in the last thirty years. His death would see me head into a number of difficult phases, but the memory of our friendship always helped pull me out. This made me see the tremendous impact we have on each other. It was a brutal lesson of how short life can be and how every minute we spend with other people matters. Whether it's building friendships in our personal lives or establishing relationships in business, with every interaction we set the stage for how people will remember us.

## CHAPTER THREE
*Your network will make all the difference*

It's not until you sit back and look, that you can genuinely appreciate all the people you have connected with and the role they played in where you are today. Whether it was their advice, inspiration or support, or maybe in some cases, the complete opposite. From the smallest of influences, to playing a significant role in life, with every person you meet it starts out the same, with a hello. Even from the shortest of chance meetings there is always something you can learn. Everyone has their own story, experiences and wisdom to share.

This is what having a network of diverse friends and acquaintances taught me. I think I was unconsciously building a network from the age of six. Even though I didn't know what that was or what purpose it served. It seemed a natural process and a necessary one to help me navigate my way through the world. It's how I got along and found my place. Today is exactly the same, from the people I meet in the surf, to business associates and cafe regulars who converge at the same time every day. If you listen, smile and offer up conversation, a meaningful connection can come from the most unlikely of people.

My life changed significantly the year Tobey died. Even though I'm no longer close with any of my friends from back then, I learnt many things hanging out with this large group. The strange thing is, this is true for all of us but most of the time we don't realise it. The networks we build around us at any age, mould and shape us into the people we are. Something I was to learn the hard way.

Compared to the party-centric fun of high school years, college felt all too serious. Aside from my obsession with sports and music, I was a woefully lazy student. None of my older siblings had finished college and from the start, I suspected I wouldn't either. I stuck it out for a little over a year before throwing in the towel.

It all came about when I found myself chatting to a friend and it suddenly felt like way too much to handle. I remember saying, "I don't think I can do this anymore. It feels like today is taking forever. How am I going to get through the next hour, the next day, let alone the rest of this year?" And for the first time in my life I felt a kind of anxiety. Time felt as though it was literally standing still.

This was the day I decided to leave college. I'd like to blame the uninspiring teachers for my misery and lack of motivation, but the blame landed squarely with me. I just wasn't getting what I thought I needed out of life. I wanted to escape the brain-numbing routine and start experiencing the world. My growing list of short-term, instantly gratifying goals became the priority, like getting my first set of wheels.

Within a month, I was working full-time at the local Superstore. Not the most prestigious of roles but it was an honest step in the existence of an employee and it sure beat doing the milk run after school. I worked hard, but the job quickly became predictable and boring for a teenager who just wanted to have fun. So, I found alternate ways to make it more enjoyable. It didn't take me long to make friends with my equally-as-bored colleagues, and soon my work situation was providing me with everything I wanted.

Throughout my school years, with every disappointing grade card, my father warned me, "You'll end up stocking shelves at a grocery store one day." And he was right, to start with anyway. While my career began with stacking shelves, I knew it wouldn't be forever. At seventeen, I felt too young to be worried about the serious things in life, like a career.

It didn't take long for me to notice however, my work colleagues held a very different view. To them this job was their life. It was serious stuff and it became the all-consuming topic of conversations around the store and at the pub after work. Becoming a manager of 'this' department or a manager of 'that' floor was the holy grail. It drove me crazy.

As much as my colleagues pined for advancement, they all obviously hated turning up to work every day. It didn't make sense. But over time, over beers and over weekend bonding sessions, their talk of being in charge and becoming a success wore me down. It came to the point where I started to sound just the same as them. Perhaps one part of me just wanted to fit in.

While I went along with the ideas they were filling my head with, most of the time I believed there had to be better things to look forward to, even for someone with a solid C average. But at that age, I only knew I wanted more, I just didn't have a clue what 'more' was, and I definitely couldn't see any obvious pathways or options to get me there.

I started applying for random jobs, which didn't get me any further than frequent rejections of my poorly written application letters. But after a couple of years of pure frustration at my lack of progress, I began to settle in where I was. And it was so easy to do. Instead of thinking for myself, I could just listen to those around me. And instead of chasing dreams, I fell under the spell of doing only what was familiar. I dealt with the numbness by spending what I earned, investments in temporary moments of fulfilment.

To satiate my lack of freedom in one part of my life, I decided to pursue it in the only way I knew how, and I moved out of my parent's house. First, I lodged with my brother, then shifted in with my cousin, before renting a place on my own. It was so easy to fall into this kind of lifestyle, and it was a lifestyle with little challenge. It was a lifestyle of ignorance. I was hypnotised by the circular nature of my existence and dulled by my routines. Every week was the same, both boring and wasteful.

Back then, I didn't really understand what it meant to think like an 'entrepreneur'. The success of others through innovation, sheer grit and determination was just not a known subject. We didn't talk about those things in my circles. Instead, all career discussions centred around our pursuit of the great 'Aussie dream', the dream of conformity and following in the footsteps of our parents. And those footsteps were clearly laid out before us.

Finishing school was the first step, then get a job, then get married, have babies, take out a mortgage, keep your job to pay off the mortgage and all the expenses that come with a picture-perfect family. However, the step that never gets mentioned is that once you have all these things and have achieved 'the dream', you then have to complain about them incessantly because it's not the life you would have chosen. If only you'd known you had a choice. This dream certainly wasn't my dream, it felt more like a bear trap. Yet I was the odd one out, like there must be something wrong with me.

The earliest image I remember of success, was of a man smartly dressed, closely shaven, slicked back hair and an 'I have it all worked out' expression on his face. I don't know where this image came from, but it stuck in my head. I always felt as though that man knew something I didn't. I started to think successful people must be very different from me. Maybe they were privileged in some way or perhaps they were simply born smarter. Success must be for other people.

Within a few years of flailing around pointlessly, I fell in with the wrong crowd. I took a few foolish turns and soon hit rock bottom. After resigning from my job, I moved to the other side of the country and continued to disappear into a dark haze. These were very bad years and the deeper I fell into this world, the less I could recognise of myself. To fund my self-indulgence, I sold everything that meant so much to me - my music collection, my hi-fi, even my guitars. I blamed everything but myself for my hopeless circumstances. By the end I had nothing, and the only way I was going to get out of the mess was if I decided to change.

Around my twenty-first birthday, my parents made the five-hour flight to come visit me for a few days. And it was shortly after this rude awakening, I decided to move back home. I had put myself through hell, physically, mentally, emotionally and financially - and I had a tremendous battle in front of me. But I had to clean myself up.

At that point I would do anything to make it happen. So, I made a commitment to myself - if I got through it, I would never squander another opportunity in my life, not ever. In many ways, I was lucky to be alive. Soon that life was well behind me and instead of being pulled down by regret, I was uplifted by self-belief. Getting through this period provided me with the motivation to do and be more.

I was incredibly grateful for the opportunity to start again. What looked from the outside to be a disastrous period of my existence had actually led me back on track, forcing a much-needed change in my life by bringing me intense clarity. I started to view life in a whole new light. Removing the limitations I once thought kept me safe, I now saw risks and opportunities from a new perspective. I started to think differently about what might be possible. I became more positive and confident about the future.

There were times when I'd joke about never making forty, but I always knew I would. I just believed everything would be okay. It was a feeling I carried with me, something I implicitly believed in. Maybe it had to do with my mother's positive influence, but I always felt good fortune was on my side, or as Tobey and I would put it, perhaps I was 'peril-resistant'.

I soon went back to the life I had before I took a wrong turn. The friends who I'd abandoned during the heavy fog, were still there waiting for me to sort my mess out. I picked life up again from where I'd left it, but this time with an almost blinding awareness of how important it was to choose the right people to surround myself with. It was time to lift my average.

## CHAPTER FOUR

*Are you looking for anything in particular?*

A year after I returned home and sorted myself out, my eldest brother arranged an interview for me at his work, a consumer electronics and musical products store in Canberra. I knew the place well; our garage band would often loan out mixing desks and amplifiers for our jam sessions. My brother was leaving for a new role interstate and he put my name forward for one of two sales jobs opening up.

In our family cabinet sat a picture of my brother in his work shirt and company tie, the same company I was applying to. My parents were so proud of him and his career success. There was no doubting his sales abilities, which all started with that consumer electronics company and eventually landed him in executive roles with some of Australia's most respected retail giants. His were big shoes to fill.

By a miracle, I got the job.

I felt confident going in on my first day, this wasn't my only attempt at being a salesperson. Before I returned to Canberra, I had a very brief role in the luxury wine industry, selling high-end product direct to the public through expos and events. With absolutely no knowledge of sales, in my first week I was put through a comprehensive training program that changed my whole perception of what sales people do.

Until this point, I'd assumed sales people were slippery and untrustworthy because they used tricks or 'gift-of-the-gab' to talk you into things you didn't need. My new boss taught me there was in fact a profession to it and a specific process. He put me through the standard sales training, ensuring I understood each step inside and out; from greeting, building rapport, qualifying, identifying and product knowledge, to handling objections and closing. But the most valuable gift he gave me came well after I could prove I'd mastered the basics - he taught me the most effective way to 'think' about making a sale, which I could apply to all sales situations.

This luxury wine salesman told me the process wasn't just about sales steps. Instead, I was to imagine each step as a fenced paddock, and it was my job to move all the sheep from paddock to paddock without leaving any sheep behind. The sheep could only be moved one-by-one as I answered all of the customer's questions and alleviated any doubt. The goal was to get all the sheep into the last paddock, where ultimately, I would close the sale.

At first it seemed like a really weird way to approach selling, but once I got my head around it, it made perfect sense.

The idea is you can't leave any sheep or doubt behind as you move through the sales steps, or you'd have to go back and get them. So, if you know your product, understand exactly what the customer needs and handle all possible objections, then there should only be one outcome; a yes. If it's a no, then you've obviously left 'sheep' behind somewhere.

The process worked and translated smoothly to consumer electronics. The more conscious I was of it, the more natural it became and the more sales I made. My personality seemed perfectly suited to this environment and as a result, I loved my job. Sales wasn't a dirty word after all. There were no tricks, just an honest simple process. And if done correctly there was no reason it couldn't be both rewarding and fun.

Above all, the sales I was making in this role taught me I could do something greater than stocking shelves. It assured me I was much more than the sum of my school grades; it strengthened the belief I had in myself.

Whilst I was always conscious of the sheep and the training I was given, one thing that stood out to me was the awkward close of a sale. I was certain there was a better way, so I developed my own approach. Instead of waiting till the end of a sale to ask the typical - "so would you like to take this one?", I started to focus on closing the sale from the very beginning. Every sheep moved through the process was further confirmation we were headed in the right direction. So as my customer progressed through the process to arrive at the point of decision, the only logical choice was to purchase; all I had to do now was shut up.

I'd completely disproved the belief that customers decide on an emotional level. Instead, the decision to purchase could be guided through agreed logic. Emotion might be part of the experience of purchasing but it wasn't the exclusive motivator. And while it may be the customer's mind which drove their emotions, it was my job to instil confidence in 'their' decision from a logical perspective. As I perfected the craft of moving sheep, I connected, listened and communicated more effectively with my customers. Closing more sales - but without the awkwardness or scripted feel of my colleagues.

My goal as a salesperson was to create a conversation which was never forced, awkward or out of place. It had to be one that gathered and maintained its momentum organically. I never talked anyone into making a purchase. I didn't need to. The only reason why you need to convince someone to buy, is if you got lazy and missed something along the way.

I believe even as salespeople, we forget just how effective people are at selling products to themselves. Many customers are already convinced of the purchase they know they want to make. I wanted my clients to never feel sold to, not ever. I wanted my customers to feel as though they had made the smart choice and be confident in their decision. And of course, be happy to return and buy from me again.

This first serious sales role kickstarted a long, successful and fulfilling career, and this sales process evolved through varied roles and exposure to new environments and experiences. It became second-nature and served to separate me from others in my industry.

Sales became my craft and the platform from which all else was built. My sales approach was simple, follow the process, be kind and be honest. If I didn't know something, I found out for myself, the best way for me to learn. And I was pleased to discover the skills needed to be great in sales seemed to come easy.

In the mid-nineties, the 'professionalism of sales' was something sales people took seriously, especially in consumer electronics. It was a super competitive field. We had to prove ourselves to earn a coveted spot on the sales floor and once we got it, it was baptism by fire. We had to be prepared to answer any question about any product. We had no choice but to learn on the go, memorising model numbers and specifications, understanding the technologies and technicalities, learning right there in front of the customer.

But the best sales people were always the ones focused on the client. I didn't want to fill my head with numbers when I could just read them on a box, so I concentrated on the area of biggest impact, knowing how to connect with the customer. I had to go right back to basics.

I had to master the simple act of listening.

Sounded easy enough, but I soon discovered there were many ways to get this wrong and only one approach that worked. It was all about empathy - the ability to detect how other people feel.

My childhood curiosity gave me a head-start on listening effectively. I was open to what other people were saying and flexible about changing my mind. Salespeople, or anyone really, can't afford to be fixed in their thinking. Sure, we can reject ideas, but the mind should always remain open. This valuable skill helped me to see and feel from someone else's perspective without being swayed by my own. This meant not only listening to the words that were being spoken but being able to feel what the customer said too.

This enabled real listening. And as I got better at this, I heard all that was being said and not said, picking up on what the customer really wanted.

Talking with someone is not hard, listening is not hard either (if you're genuinely interested). However, when you are selling products, selling yourself, managing relationships, negotiating, dealing with problems or conflict, there is an added layer of complexity to basic communication. Everything is heightened when the stakes get higher. Everything we say or don't say, just as everything we do or fail to do, can have a tremendous impact.

The longer I spent in sales, the more sensitive I became to the complexity of the signals people send, especially when I eventually transferred my retail sales skills into the corporate environment. Through countless conversations, meetings and interviews I recognised just how important it was to not only read these signals accurately but be conscious of the ones I was sending myself.

I first heard about reading people from my great-uncle Bob. He had an interesting theory about people and the signals they unwittingly send. I always held an unwavering respect for Bob, he was a true English gentleman, intelligent, articulate and incredibly funny, and every time we sat down to chat, I would learn something new.

A successful business man, Bob relocated from the UK to Australia where he had been general manager of a global brand. Bob's closest friends included some of Australia's most prominent and pioneering retailers.

As someone who would've held a thousand meetings throughout his life, when I started taking my sales career seriously, I asked to pick his brain. And although he had only one gem to share, it stuck with me and raised my awareness of every movement people make.

"When I interviewed someone Chris, I could learn more from watching them walk out of the room, than from what they said when they sat down in front of me".

At first, I thought he was kidding but I've come to believe this can be incredibly accurate. So much of what we say about ourselves is hidden in tiny gestures and movements. And they reveal more than any carefully delivered words can. If you look closely you can read the smallest of movements in others and recognise them in yourself. Awareness of this is essential, especially in high pressure situations where we reveal even more if we aren't confident in what we're doing.

After Bob and I discussed sales for a little bit longer, I asked him about my girlfriend at the time. He replied, "Nice girl - but Chris, that walk…"

# CHAPTER FIVE
*The biggest failure is to not take risks*

A couple of years into my first sales job, I asked to apply for a store manager role. I enjoyed working in my current position, but something told me I had to do it. Suddenly I was thrust into a completely different world. When I got the keys, it was a real 'wow' moment. I was filled with a sense of achievement, an unexpected and addictive feeling, one that would change me and my relationship to work. It was a feeling I would try and replicate over and over again throughout my career.

    I would've stopped at nothing to make my store a success and make my boss proud. But with no management experience and limited support, I had to learn on the fly. It didn't take long for that sense of achievement to wear off. Most of my days were spent bundled up in the office preparing reports, counselling staff or dealing with some other issue. I accepted everything was my problem to fix - I was learning after all.

    In just a few short months, I went from care-free salesman, smiling and laughing my way through the day, to an overflowing in-tray of paperwork and stuff I didn't really understand. I never once stopped and thought to myself that management was not my thing. I didn't question it once. Instead I fell into line and forgot my instinct to question everything.

Deep down, I probably didn't feel as though I deserved it. So, I swallowed feelings of inadequacy by doing what was expected of me. But when I focused only on sales, it felt like I was working on something for myself. Sure, I was making money for someone else, but sales was my craft and all the tools I needed to do a great job were in my head. I had unintentionally traded this source of freedom, as though climbing the ladder was my only option to get ahead.

Looking back, my old views on career progression were naive. I always assumed the harder I worked, the higher I'd climb. And the higher I'd climb, the more money I'd make. And of course, the more money I'd make, the happier I'd become. I didn't grow up in a wealthy family, so I honestly didn't know any better. All I ever experienced was when I had money in my pocket, it made me happy.

I spent the next couple of years as a manager in Canberra before heading off to Sydney, where my learning curve became dangerously vertical as I dealt with a multitude of store issues. It was an incredibly stressful time, far removed from the fun I'd enjoyed working on the sales floor. The fact is, I was built for sales not for management. All of my wiring, life experiences and natural talent was directed toward sales where I found the most joy. I ran that store for a year or so before the whole company closed operations.

I moved back to Canberra and picked up a role with a different company. This time it would be different, purely sales again, no management responsibilities. I was free of the burdens, and as it turned out the pay was even better than the previous management job

I'd suffered through. I now had time to relax after work, time to get fit and enjoy my days off. Evenings and weekends were once again full of social events as everything clicked back in to place. For a short while anyway.

My manager at the time was keen to see me progress, rewarding me for my efforts by planting motivational seeds. And like Jack to the Beanstalk, I found the idea irresistible.

At first, he just asked me to be a department manager, where I handled all the purchasing and negotiations with suppliers, ran the inventory and managed the sales floor. He made sure I had this under control before grooming me for my own store, a highly sought-after proprietorship. And just as before, I was happy to give away anything for it. As if the possibility of more money dwarfed all other concerns or common sense.

I remember the day I realised there was no going back. My manager took me on a road trip to a real-estate agent where he handed over a $100,000 cheque as a deposit on another investment house. I can't blame him though, when it came to money, I was an easy sell. He loved the business he was in and I was blind to the obvious negatives. So, I decided, why not give it a go? If he can do it, then I can too.

Becoming a proprietor was the holy-grail in my industry. It was a role 'every go-getter in Australia wanted', earning 'salaries like surgeons', well, that's what I was led to believe. This was all the motivation I needed. Imagine how proud my parents would be if I 'owned' my own store. I thought about what I could do with all of that money and all the happiness I would have.

Soon after meeting with the senior decision makers, I got the call and an offer of a Sydney-based store. With the advice of my boss running through my head, "if you ever get offered a store, take it, or you may not get offered one again", I naively said yes without a second thought. I didn't know what I was in for, I knew only about doing the job and managing a store, that was enough for me to be comfortable with my choice.

My decision was motivated by dreams of money, not the work I was really passionate about. And so, it turned out to be a complete disaster. Despite a few good days, the store was plagued by theft, most of it internal, the books were a mess and the staff were less motivated than a bear in winter. I'd inherited an absolute lemon.

Within weeks, my gut told me it wasn't the right choice, but the lure of the 'surgeon's-wage' kept me hanging in with the hope of something prosperous around the corner. And therein lay the problem. I was caught within a machine. And this very machine dangled the carrots that kept me labouring away uselessly without reward. It was soul-stripping but the pride I held for what I had accomplished and the desire for more success, trumped any instinct to give up. Instead of having the guts to walk away, I pushed on and told myself it's just the way it is. I had no choice but to suck it up.

I was convinced that life and success were meant to be hard. It must be this way because without a degree how else was I going to earn the big bucks? So, I gave it my all, I worked long hours, six, seven days a week. On the rare occasions when I'd finally get some rest, I'd be woken by security alarm call outs, often several times a night. I'd arrive at the store to find busted windows or empty shelves behind smashed display cabinets. The store became a recurring nightmare. It got to the point where I'd wake up most mornings dreading what would be waiting for me when I'd pull up for work.

The stresses of the business didn't stop at the edge of the carpark either. I remember my first appearance as a new proprietor at the steering committee, where I was flanked by far more experienced proprietors and business people who'd been in their seats for many years. The General Manager at the time, leered at me through the top of his glasses. I felt like a kid in school as he scolded me over a foolish comment, "Why would you say that?" What was worse than the scolding however, was he actually wanted an answer. The room was full of new colleagues and my heart sunk. I couldn't stop thinking to myself, "What am I doing here…?".

Once I got over the embarrassment of my first error, I never made it again. It sparked my desire to learn to be like them, to be the very best at what I did. At the next meeting, the GM said to me, still leering through the top of his glasses but now with a grin, "Good Chris, now we're doing business". Like drinking from a fire-hydrant, there was a whole other side to this industry I was desperately soaking in at a rapid pace. From learning what to say and when to say it, to understanding leverage in the complex world of negotiations. What one day seemed foreign and confusing, appeared logical and natural the next. I began to change the way I thought about work and how I approached the job. I wasn't on the sales floor anymore; I wasn't down in the trenches. It required a new way of thinking and I haven't looked at business in the same way since.

Regrettably, I lasted as a proprietor just a few years, and aside from the many business and life lessons I gained, I left no richer and certainly no happier. I also didn't leave until it had completely turned my personal life upside-down and inside-out. From marriage to divorce, praise and euphoria to anxiety and stress, it was a period of drama with very little reprieve.

Despite all I learned, there were only two standout positives I took with me from this period. They were the ability to do business in the boardroom and the newly found pastime of surfing. It was a ride I thought I could've done without - but in the end it served to only strengthen my character.

Even though I had my share of success, at the exact moment of walking away it felt like I was admitting to the world I was an absolute failure. But I couldn't have been more wrong. As it turned out this was the smartest decision I could've made, my only regret was it should have come earlier. I had no job to go to and no home, aside from a mate's couch, but I chose to use this opportunity to start again and to not panic.

For the moment, I wasn't chasing money or ideas of 'success', I instead focused on rebuilding my life, starting with the things I was most passionate about. While it took lots of hard work to secure that franchise, it took simple intelligence to walk away. The choice was a moral one and in the end it had very little to do with success or lack thereof.

I had to come to terms with my mistakes and recognise where I'd stuffed up in life. Otherwise I'd be doomed to repeat it. I had to make peace with it, to move on, be happy and feel free. Unemployed and broke, but happy and free.

I'm forever grateful to the mate who helped me out just when I needed it most. A fellow ex-proprietor, he created a role for me at his new store. It was my salvation, as I was down to my last dollar. Although it wasn't my ultimate career goal, I didn't care, it meant there was no hurry for me to work everything out. I wasn't making a ton of money, but I had everything I needed, my Jeep, my hi-fi and a growing quiver of surfboards. Instead of feeling regret or failure at the life I'd left behind, it helped me feel empowered.

Within a few months, I made drastic but necessary changes to my lifestyle and found myself living with a couple of hippies down on the coast of southern Sydney. I hadn't tasted this kind of freedom in a long time. I'd missed so much of life when I was so tightly wrapped. I'd forgotten what it felt like to just have fun. Without the stresses, everything took on a new meaning. There was an inner happiness and positivity I carried around with me. Everything started to turn around.

Now I was working more humane hours, I began spending most of my mornings and days-off at the beach. One of my reps was a keen surfer and he regularly invited me over to the Northern Beaches of Sydney to join him for a surf. He lived in a classic beach house, perched on the top of the headlands overlooking one of Sydney's great breaks. I fell in love with his Northern Beaches lifestyle. Many times, I'd make the long trip north so we could explore the coast, searching for quieter spots to spend a few hours in the waves before returning to his place for a couple of cold beers whilst overlooking the ocean.

Surfing became so important to me during this period. It allowed me to escape, to relax, think and breathe. And what started out as a passing interest and a healthy distraction, ended up forcing me to revaluate what I really wanted out of life. Surfing was the exact potion I needed. Just being there in the salt with a mate, that's what it was all about. This land-locked Canberra boy who'd spent most of his life with his feet firmly planted on the ground, fell in love with the feeling of the ocean's power beneath him.

Once I settled into my new working lifestyle, I realised that chasing success had come at a heavy cost. Along the way I'd somehow lost touch with myself, my positivity and my confidence - the natural me. I'd stopped exploring possibilities and stopped asking questions. I'd allowed myself to feel trapped as though I had no choice, when in actual fact all I had was choice.

In the end what I needed was to let go. Just walk away. The franchise dream was just that, a dream - an ill-informed dream. Realising this enabled me to take the most significant risks in search of the biggest payoffs.

After all my years in retail, I had a number of loyal customers who I'd help from time to time. One in particular, needed an audio system for his bar in Manly. He asked me about my new situation and quickly learned I'd been through a difficult patch. His suggestion was to come work for him at the pub a few nights a week, "It'll be good for you", he said. Even though I lived over ninety minutes away, I needed the extra cash.

If it'd been twelve months earlier, I wouldn't have been interested, not in the slightest. But I was in a different place now and the idea of working in a pub somehow attracted me. Perhaps it was the idea of doing something completely different, maybe it was the opportunity to meet new people. Either way, he knew exactly what I needed.

On my first night, he greeted me at the door, threw me a shirt and said, "Put that on and follow me". It was only nine o'clock, but the bar was already packed, and he headed straight for it. I was terrified - I'd never pulled a beer in my life. We walked in through the back area and just as I was about to breathe a sigh of relief, he pushed open the door to the main bar. Suddenly I was under ultra-bright lights with music blaring. Twenty or thirty customers were all queuing up at the bar that I now stood behind. He turned to me, winked and said, "Here you go, enjoy mate", before disappearing into the smoke-filled room.

There was no time to ask questions or panic. I quickly made friends with one of the other bar staff, who kindly gave me a ten-minute power tour, before I started pulling my first beer. There was no point fighting it, I just had to go with the flow. I quickly forgot about the extra money I was earning. It turned out the social benefits were what I enjoyed and needed the most. It helped bring me out of my shell again, it gave me a new challenge and made me positively uncomfortable.

I realised the only place I was trapped was in my head. It was by far the most rewarding aspect of the job. Knowing I had options gave me powerful psychological leverage. I realised now that if everything turned to shit, I could always go work in a pub. So, there was nothing to fear, nothing to worry about. I was doing the exact thing I avoided since my first retail job. I was doing something unknown, something I had to learn from scratch, something I knew nothing about. I was exploring options and falling in love with the new found freedom. My confidence was restored.

Working behind the bar and the people I met, led me on many new experiences. I was taking risks and saying yes to people more often, sometimes to things that previously didn't interest me. I just wanted to see what else was out there. Life quickly became the adventure I craved, decisions were made on the spot and I did whatever I felt like doing. For me, this is where the excitement in life comes from - through new experiences, people and taking chances.

My friend at the pub had done me a huge favour. After all those stressful years when I'd felt pushed to the edge of my sanity, I'd never really felt in control. But having options suddenly gave me a sense of control. Instead of being governed by career or monetary security, I enjoyed taking a chance on myself and testing old comfort zones.

I eventually saved enough to pay down the remaining debts from my franchise days and rented a tiny apartment on the Northern Beaches. It was a haven. I found a great balance of socialising, surfing, working in my day job and now pulling beers on weekends. I felt completely free and I didn't miss the franchise, not one bit. That old life, the one I'd once strived for, seemed more like a bad dream. Thankfully, one I woke myself up from.

It's amazing to think about how much of my attitude shifted thanks to the random decision to work at a pub. Within just a few months my life was transformed. The risk of doing something completely out of the ordinary had paid off.

Life became about embracing the random opportunities now available to me. Without them, life seemed predictable and boring. I began to see randomness as one of life's greatest gifts. It was the unexpected source of excitement and new experiences. It was everywhere I went and in all the people I met.

Countless opportunities began opening up, including opportunities to change. This came in both how I was thinking and in what I believed about the world. When I embraced the randomness, I developed trust in myself, I accepted 'what is'. This was a powerful and centring stress-reducer for my life. I worked out that if I couldn't control it or influence it, it was best to just let it go.

Even though I enjoyed working at my mate's store, the three-hour round trip to my day job was a killer, especially when I was pulling beers well into weekend mornings before backing it up on the sales floor the same day. I needed something more in line with the life I wanted.

I decided it was time to get off the retail floor, so I applied for a corporate job, in sales, of course. It was a representative role, working for a family-owned company, selling communication products business to business. The manager and the owner were relaxed and very approachable. They both had a non-corporate and down-to-earth energy I was immediately drawn to.

I got the feeling during the interview that I would get the job, it felt like the sort of place I could make an impact. Once I fluked the psychometric test, I accepted the position and handed in my resignation from my mate's store. In just a few months, I was settled enough to also stop working at the pub. The corporate sales role gave me the new experience of weekends to myself, which after years in retail I never had the opportunity to enjoy. And now nothing was going to interfere with spending my Saturdays and Sundays down the beach.

The role seemed too good to be true. But after a few short months, it started to feel as though I was really meant to be there. It had everything I was looking for, autonomy, higher pay and loads of future potential. The business had a great culture and the people were fun to work with.

If I hadn't decided it was time to cut the cord and leave the shop floor, I never would have discovered this was exactly what I should be doing. This new sales role would catapult me toward the kind of success I couldn't have imagined when I bought into the franchise dream - the largest failure I had experienced in life so far, had in fact led me to what would be my largest financial rewards.

## CHAPTER SIX

*Be comfortable with being uncomfortable*

I was a high-achieving salesperson, who suddenly had to start at the bottom. No longer in a position where the customers came to me, I had to go out and find the customers and sell them the idea of giving me their time. The world of business to business sales was a very different beast. I knew no one in this industry and no one knew who the hell I was. But my competitive streak would not let me stay at the bottom for long.

I'm competitive at pretty much everything, from kicking the footy to securing deals. I've often refused to accept I couldn't win, I believed there was always a way. My friends often joke about it, but it's been a part of me from a young age. Competitiveness can be a healthy trait, even a fun one if you know how to harness it for the right reasons. But I learned the hard way that I wasn't infallible.

As a kid, I often reaped the rewards of the positive streak underlying my sometimes-cocky competitiveness, but the first time I totally bombed publicly, it shocked some sense into me. At my debut state Judo tournament, in the under forty-four kilo class, I went in too confident, believing I knew all the techniques and all I had to do was execute them. My only part in this knock-out competition lasted just thirty seconds. My opponent grabbed me aggressively and with a perfect shoulder throw pinned me to the mat. My back screamed in pain and I was finished for the rest of the event. I was completely out of my league.

It came as a rude awakening. I might have done all the training over many years, but when I faced off, I was completely unprepared. I felt as though I had suddenly entered the real world and asked myself, "Where am I? What is this place?" This monumental failure (it felt monumental at that age) held a great lesson for me, it taught me the value of experience, knowledge and what a genuine desire to win really is. It also motivated me to never again feel that sort of embarrassment. I realised, despite my public pinning, the only place to learn how to fight, was on the mat.

When I was in my teens, I hated being beaten at anything and I turned my hand to all sports, just to prove to myself I could compete. For every new sport and skill I wanted to excel at, I knew there would always be a first time I had to go in as the least experienced. But until I got through the initiation, I couldn't possibly progress to the next level. The reward was, this competitiveness would eventually influence my professional career.

Inexperience working in business to business sales may have started me off on the back-foot, but my competitiveness wouldn't allow me to accept anything less than giving it my best shot. I absorbed every little piece of information in an effort to be better than what was expected. I chose to let my inexperience bring a new perspective to corporate sales, by trawling my previous experience for any advantage.

My early sales career taught me that competitiveness wasn't about being the best salesperson on the floor, or about making more sales than everyone else. Being competitive meant understanding that the only person you're in competition with is yourself.

The first time I heard the words, "just do your best", was not when most people would expect. The competitive environment I grew up in had me believing I wouldn't reach my best until I came out on top. But my first sales manager was the only person who feigned to teach me otherwise.

When I first heard those words, "just do your best", I realised there were two sides to how this encouragement could work. Firstly, I thought he was saying that if I didn't achieve the targets but did my best, then that's all he could reasonably ask. And this was all I could ask of myself. The effort was in my hands. It was up to me to define what doing my best would look like.

Secondly, this made me see that winning isn't everything. But doing your best is. You can be satisfied at the end of the day if you put in your best effort, even if you don't come out on top. However, I think this applies to winning too, because a win achieved with a half-arsed effort is nowhere near as rewarding as one from which you excelled against yourself.

Winning doesn't always mean you did your best. It means you finished first and others lost. There's a distinct difference. I recall running the one-hundred metres at school. Whilst I'd run hard, it wasn't until I could hear the footsteps of someone getting close that I really put in the extra effort. When pushed, we are capable of more than we otherwise produce, but if we can harness this motivation, we can achieve more than we expect.

Winning is beating your personal best, that's the real competition. I'm competitive in business because I don't ever want to settle or wait until I hear footsteps coming up from behind. Many people just exert the minimum effort required to land somewhere around the top. But starting a new role in corporate sales, it wouldn't be enough for me to just get by or finish first. I had to extend myself further than ever before.

"If he can do it, then I can do it too", was the most valuable belief about competitiveness I carried with me since playing sport as a kid. I just couldn't accept there might be something out of my reach. I never saw a difference between myself and other people, just the difference of mindset or time spent gaining experience and developing my own techniques.

The only person that can place limitations on an individual, is the individual. I found if anyone even suggested there was a limitation on my ability to perform, my response was always to challenge it. Anytime I put myself out there and did my best, I would always learn more about myself, win or lose. And every time I lost - and there were some spectacular ones, I came out of it knowing exactly what I needed to work on.

This became essential knowledge for me in those critical first months in corporate sales, I thrived only because I understood the importance of how to use my competitiveness to evolve and adapt. All I had to do was work out how the other guys did it, so I could do it too. Only better.

In the corporate world there was always other business people who were more articulate, more educated, more intelligent and who earned a lot more than me. It would have been all too easy to get caught up in the politics and power plays, allowing myself to get intimidated by someone's stature or the position stated on their business card. I had to remind myself - everyone has to start somewhere. That first year, I was in my 'somewhere'.

The sooner I really understood everyone 'puts their pants on one leg at a time', the sooner I began to relax in big meetings and presentations. Anyone can connect with another human being when they open their eyes to the fact that at some point, we are all the same. The more a person embraces this, the more likely they are to be themselves, especially in high pressure situations.

I began to get comfortable with the idea of being uncomfortable as I faced a huge learning curve with only my confidence and enthusiasm to back me. I could very easily have turned and ran from the challenge of a completely new industry and the intimidating buyers who saw straight through my shiny new business cards and the only suit my meagre budget could afford. But I persisted.

I turned many upfront 'no's into certain and long-lasting 'yes's in my first few years at this company. I built business relationships and personal friendships with people who had much higher standing in the industry, all because I didn't allow myself to believe I was any different from them. We all have our own experiences, but we also have our own version or way to do things, and therefore, our own value to contribute. Once I recognised what my personal strengths were, I could utilise them to build my own success.

Corporate life, unlike the sales floor, began to teach me how to embrace new occasions of being uncomfortable and to not fear them. They became opportunities to grow in real time. I could learn from the stalwarts of the industry, regardless of who they were, the more powerful and untouchable they appeared, the better. I found that being uncomfortable became a clear indicator I was putting in real effort. Where some may shrivel up and avoid these situations, I used them to my advantage.

My work in corporate sales was going extremely well, I was having successes where others before me had failed. I brought a fresh perspective on who we were selling the product to and I wanted to see the product in major retail. Aided by my years of experience and knowledge of the retail business and culture, I understood everything surrounding the product's potential success or failure.

During my earlier years in the role, I found myself travelling around Australia to train our major retailers on our newly launched products. Little did I know I was presenting to the future love of my life when I reached Adelaide. A part-time retail sales rep and fashion designer, I could tell she had a good heart from the moment we met. During the training session I was concentrating mostly on how to convince this girl to come out for a drink with me. One round of drinks for everyone after the training and my plan had worked. Within a few months she'd moved to Sydney, where we lived together and eventually married. She has become the most important person in my life.

It felt as though I had stumbled across a secret formula - at the time, I remember saying to my mother, "I finally worked it out Mum", which was the twenty-something version of "look Mum, no hands". I was doing the work I loved and had time to surf every day. As my sense of success grew stronger and stronger, I felt untouchable again, like I was creating my own luck and the good times would just keep coming.

The transition from selling to consumers, to selling to business became easier, as I saw the many parallels and skills that lent to both. Over a period of time, we created the opportunity to focus on selling only one brand, and with this shift, I was able to further sharpen my skills. This newly evolved role allowed me to extend my sales ability into the field of long-term relationship management, and it was here I discovered my true career calling.

Over the next year or so, we created a whole new sales channel for the company and hired a dedicated team in support. We all worked hard to grow this part of the business into a success. The owners were smart and inspiring to work for. And although I found it easy to be extremely passionate about the work, mostly I think I wanted to thank them for taking a chance on me.

After a few years, a new product was about to be launched by the brand I was focused on. Their new technology was in high demand, it was a dream scenario for a salesperson, great product and perfect timing. My team quickly became instrumental in their Australian successes as we leveraged the heck out of it to grow our retail channel dramatically.

As part of the strategy to strengthen our relationship with this major brand, I was given the opportunity to travel to the US to see their operations. I wasn't surprised to find a team of dedicated and passionate people behind the products, everyone from the top down had this contagious energy and drive. However, it was during one of these trips I realised, if they decided to change their strategy and take this business over, all they had to do was step in. All of my hard work could disappear in a millisecond. They could take the sales and all I had built.

Surprisingly, this didn't happen, well not in the way I'd imagined. Coincidentally, there came about some staffing changes in the team at work, including the appointment of a new marketing manager. We didn't click from the beginning and what started as a simple difference of opinion, quickly escalated into an issue that drove a wedge between the GM and me. I was deeply saddened by the effect on the professional relationship I treasured, one we regrettably never had the opportunity to restore.

The workplace and sales role I loved, eventually became a source of frustration. The changing energies at work threw my once serene life completely out of balance.

However, instead of everything turning to shit, the brand I'd worked so hard to make a national success decided it was time to hire someone locally to run the retail business. Even though my biggest fears had come true, I was in a position to apply for the role, and I got it.

Delivering the unexpected news of my resignation to the owners was a horrible experience. But all I could do was remind myself, in their own way they'd already made the decision for me. They just weren't aware of it.

What I didn't know however, I was also making a fatal choice.

Within a few short weeks, I found myself working for one of the world's leading tech companies. I felt like I was getting recognition for the years of hard work that launched this brand successfully into Australian retail. Now I had the added freedom to build on what I'd already created.

We set about transforming the local model and the successes continued. All of my experience, skills and passion were blending into one. The role was challenging, and I needed to make sure I grew with it. I took advantage of every opportunity to expand my knowledge of the entire business, learning new skills that became essential for my future, from production to PR and everything in between.

Working remotely from a home office, I was allowed to maintain the autonomy I had enjoyed over the last few years, flying interstate and overseas for meetings when needed. I found the lack of office distractions enabled me to focus and develop greater discipline and self-motivation. And for a while there, it was the perfect role.

I worked mostly solo on the retail side of the business for many years, travelling most weeks and managing a business with several major accounts, including one of the company's largest internationally. We grew very fast, in fact so fast it got to the point where I could go for weeks without a surf. I was extremely proud but working tirelessly, late into most nights and weekends, whatever was needed to make this brand a success. Before long, the pressure to keep up with the demands of such a business began to dominate my world.

What I'd created was starting to consume me. I couldn't switch it off. It was all I thought about, all I read, studied and planned for. I was setting higher expectations on myself than my employer ever hinted at and I was achieving them. I desperately wanted everyone I met at that organisation to be proud to have me on the team. And with good reason, I was inspired by many of them, my direct manager and the VP's included.

This was the first time I had been given this level of responsibility in any business and I fought every instinct to pull back or step away. This was a job I could do, and more than anything I wanted to be successful. So, I made many compromises and excuses just to ensure I was never beaten and never lost an opportunity.

I qualified for international sales awards a number of times, which sent me and my wife on paid trips around the globe to some incredible locations. Every bit of heart I had to offer went in to this business and within a few short years I was exhausted but incredibly satisfied.

When my wife and I sat at the 'President's table' at the company 'world-class' sales event in Hawaii one year, it suddenly dawned on me - I did this. The person selected to sit with the President's family was no random choice. He'd picked me to be there. While it filled me with pride, it was my sense of belonging that was most powerful. Since my first day on the shop floor, some decades earlier, I had done the hard yards and it was now paying off. I was an important part of something.

There was never a moment in those first years when I didn't feel completely appreciated and rewarded for all the hard work. I was punching well above my weight in all aspects. I didn't place any limits on what I could achieve, how much work I should do and when I would do it. I treated the business as though it were my own. I rose to every occasion, overcoming any fears and proving myself over and over to eliminate all self-doubt. However, I started to sense the corporate landscape was not one I was built to succeed in.

I had so many moments of 'pinch-yourself' success, I ignored the corporate beast that would eventually sneak up on me. Hemmed in by MBA educated colleagues, I absorbed their metaphors, energy, enthusiasm and experience - until I felt like one of them.

I tried my best to remove myself from and ignore the typically structured, restrictive environment that can come with such a large organisation. But I began to feel limited and caged. Some find the structure of a procedural culture comforting and secure, whereas others can't. For most of my working life I sat somewhere between the two, before realising almost too late where I really belonged.

By this time, we'd settled into the Northern Beaches lifestyle. We lived in an apartment overlooking the beach, where we could see the sunrise over the ocean every day. I was having success at work and in life, travelling the world for business and pleasure, going to all extremes to make surfing a priority. I started living a more adventurous life again.

My surfboard was always part of my luggage ensemble as I'd quietly tag personal days onto business trips, to surf in new locations every few months. From the deserts of Las Vegas to the coast of Mexico, from wintery London to sunny Biarritz, I weathered the taunts of airline staff in landlocked airports all in the pursuit of my real destination. I began to think I'd achieved everything I would ever need. I felt I'd reached a new level of success, beyond a job well done. And on the days when I'd paddle out to experience an unexplored break, I would often feel in complete balance.

But this was the exception. The soon to be rare exception.

Home from the trip to Hawaii and back into the pace of normal life, the heaviness of expectations I placed on myself began putting a weight of stress over my working days and nights. A short year later and my work went from the peak of my passion to an all-consuming mess. Both physically and mentally, I had allowed it to take over my life. I was worn out, stressed and often felt on the brink of a much-needed breakdown. I couldn't escape it and the frequent surfing holidays I would take in an effort to recharge provided no release as the dark clouds lurked just hours away.

In the end, what drove me to leave this role was one decision made against my better judgement and intuition. It was a simple decision that set a series of events in motion, all of which I could see coming, but was powerless to stop.

# CHAPTER SEVEN
*Recognise you're the square peg*

A 'square peg in a round hole' is a person who doesn't quite fit into a situation. It definitely does not mean there is something wrong with the individual, it just implies there is a mismatch for some reason. Being a square peg in a round-hole is an expected part of the career search process. Many people simply ignore this fact or mistakenly put huge amounts of emotional energy into trying to change themselves. A smarter use of energy is to recognise your personal strengths and not focus on overcoming weaknesses in order to fit into any hole. Especially as these 'defined' spaces change over time.

From both retail and the corporate world, I was certain that excellent salespeople make poor managers, and excellent managers make poor salespeople. To be great in sales, you need to be able to understand and respond to people at a deep empathetic level, whereas I found that as I began to step into a management role again, more and more I was expected to be apathetic. It didn't sit well with me to have competing values in this way, but it came with the badge.

It's difficult to find, but I think any career functions best in an environment where there is a stable balance of power and responsibility. If managers are given the freedom to innovate and create, they have the necessary room to succeed, fail and learn. There can be a harmony when the formula is right, when the machine is humming, and everyone contributes their unique strengths to the goals of the team. But sometimes even in successful teams, things don't always get to work this way. Or something happens that upsets the balance and things begin to change. It is inevitable.

It started to change in our perfect machine, when the Australasian region had a shift in management and again when we hired new blood to work underneath me in the retail team. Circumstances began to offer increased frustrations. Our country manager would often say to me, "only worry about things in your sphere of influence Chris" and that's good advice, but my sphere of influence barely covered half of what I was responsible for. This lack of control became progressively difficult to deal with.

Repeatedly I was being asked to fall-in with the company line. To go against my instincts. And every time I did, I left behind any sense of fairness and balance, for the 'greater good' of the team. The slippery slope of the greater good didn't gel with the kind of manager I wanted to be and before too long, I couldn't go along with it anymore. I was used to working with a great deal of initiative and I placed enormous trust in my instincts. But I wasn't able to use them. What was good enough to build a business, was no longer required to maintain it under this new structure.

I knew working for a public company would be different. I expected more pressure, more reports and more forecasting. But I hadn't considered how greatly the reporting structures would begin to impact other areas. My world began to move strictly in quarters as I felt the creativity and freedom being sucked out of my work. Everything I did was about comfort zones and 'what we've always done'. It was no longer the vibrant successful retail brand we had created, it felt like it now belonged to someone else, who saw the brand from a completely different perspective than we did.

I tried as best as I could, but it simply didn't make sense anymore.

Instead of doing the things I did best, I was up until all hours sweating over spreadsheets, expense claims and monthly sales reports. The inspiration I felt when I first joined, was wiped out by tighter controls, an increase in expectations and now panicked shareholders adding pressure over the global financial crisis. It felt like our energy was being invested in all the wrong areas. It was infuriating. I'd been swallowed up by the corporate giant and didn't even realise I'd became part of its digestive system.

I even started to accept the line-toeing in justification of how much I had changed to fit into the vision of corporate success. It wasn't until I began to receive coaching to help me through a particularly stressful period, that I could see just how skewed my perspective had become. I excused the circumstances in which I found myself by valuing what I collected along the way. I'd believed the sales awards, the European car, the expensive suits and frequent overseas holidays actually mattered. But somewhere along the way, I must have swallowed the wrong pill, the blue instead of the red. My significant awakening came when an innocent joke with a colleague resulted in what I can only explain as a deeply offensive outcome.

My wife started a small side project a few years earlier, selling organic t-shirts and women's fashion. It was a labour of love she spent her free time on. My wife ran the business and I helped out when I could.

Word of the project got around the office and I was summoned by the Manager. I was told it was both a conflict of interest and breach of contract. The meeting was all bizarre and totally out of character, but he was serious. Somehow, the effort, long hours, energy and success - they all meant nothing. But organic t-shirts did? This was the push I needed, and I decided the time had come.

Some round holes can accommodate a square peg, but in my experience, they sure as hell like to make it uncomfortable for them while they are there.

My role suddenly felt completely artificial. I was disconnected from something I used to feel so deeply connected too. The freedom I used to feel in the job disappeared in an instant. It became overwhelmingly obvious to me, and I think to others in the company, that I simply didn't fit in anymore. The neatly packaged space I once enjoyed had distorted beyond comfort. It didn't matter what had been or what could be. What really mattered to me was what was happening now. I knew it was nothing to do with my ability or my achievements, but yet it had the strange sensation of somehow being personal. I didn't want to leave all my hard work behind, but things had changed and soon came an opportunity to take a little of it with me.

During the preceding twelve months, the company I worked for had purchased a well-known audio brand. My passion and background in audio saw me eagerly take over its sales in Australia. It was a timely reminder of the carefree fun times back in my first sales role. We instantly made some much-needed changes to the business, doubling the revenue within the first six months as a result. This new product line and the added responsibilities turned into an opportunity to part ways with my present frustrations as, serendipitously, after only one year the audio brand was earmarked for sale in an effort to recover losses during the GFC.

I was one of the few given the opportunity to stay with the current company or go with the new owners. The information trickling down from the senior team was that the new owners were a well-positioned private equity group, a 'family-orientated' company, who would take care of existing employees as they built a wonderful new future for the brand. It sounded like the exact change I needed; this was my out.

On a trip to China, when I had my final meeting with the VP of sales for the company I had already decided to leave, I desperately wanted to tell him all of my frustrations, but I knew it wouldn't change my situation or help things return to 'normal'. In this meeting he told me how the transition would take place and said if I decided to go, he would respect my decision, but would take me back in a heartbeat. This vote of confidence meant a lot to me, but my decision was made.

I've often thought about my choice and wondered how things might have been different if I'd tried harder to fit in. Perhaps this is what having an MBA gives you. Maybe I was too head-strong. But deep down, I don't think I would've lasted much longer anyway. To this point, I'd spent my life propagating my independence and ability to work differently. It was a part of my character, it's who I was, it had brought me success and helped me grow and I wasn't about to change that.

Within a few months under the new owners, everything returned to normal. My work-life balance came back, we were driving the business our way, and had the support and trust of management. During this time, our region became one of the most profitable in the world and although we had our share of global issues the mood was positive as we looked forward to better times.

But the better times never came.

Within a year, sales started falling dramatically in every market. We went from saying 'music's in our blood', to bleeding money. Some placed blame squarely on the products, saying they were over-engineered and over-designed, but it was a combination of factors, mostly due to the boom in 'personal audio'. As the market shifted, our recognisable brand stood still. Where we once towered over other brands, we were now just one of many in the industry and they all beat us to the punch.

In a last-ditch attempt to save the business, the senior folks took the foolish step of forcing us into a new structure, from which there would be no return. I predicted where it was going to lead and campaigned hard against it, but there was nothing I could say or do. It was head-scratching to us and others in the industry, but it was clear the new owners had brought and tried to run a business they didn't fully understand. And many good people suffered because of this.

My colleague and I worked tirelessly to persevere within the new structure dictated by our nervous owners. But instead of leading and forging new ground, we were stuck holding the hands of an inexperienced and under-gunned distributor. We did all we could to push them in the right direction, but it was a big ship to turn around, so things went from bad to worse. As I'd accurately predicted, our distributor became careless under the stress of the changing industry and their inaction resulted in a dramatic loss of business. And we had been completely stripped of any power to change it. Then came the ill-fated trip to Las Vegas, which soon left a bad taste in everyone's mouth, and any trust between us stayed behind in that stinky hotel room.

It didn't really matter how hard we fought, globally the whole organisation was heading for a crash. Within a few months the entire sales team in North America were handed redundancies and soon, not one region was spared from the brutality of protecting 'investor's money'. The 'family values' had disappeared in the panic.

Between the rumours and other erratic decisions, we could sense what was coming. The few sales people left in Europe began jumping ship and it didn't take long before we received notification of our redundancies. We were left stunned, holding tightly to the memory of once glorious opportunity, with hardly anything to show for it. Shortly after, the brand name was sold and now its rich heritage is just a faint memory in audio history.

The only thing I was sure about in this moment, was my hard work over the last ten years was too valuable to be ignored, thrown away, or rated quarter by quarter. I spent all these years investing in someone else's business, someone else's success and someone else's interests. Toeing the corporate line had gotten me nowhere. I was really good at the specific skills that brought other people success, but I failed to see it early enough.

When my tiny redundancy pay-out came through, it was an odd, confusing feeling. I felt pissed off by the treatment, trapped by my expensive lifestyle, yet somehow relieved and free to move into whatever I wanted to. I was a square peg with no hole to drop into and I was proud of it.

The suits who should've known better had unexpectedly driven me to a point of surprising freedom. My days were now empty of mindless reports and number crunching, so I turned to the surf for reconnection. It was the one source that had consistently helped me block out the stresses and anger. It was here I could switch it all off and just be in the moment.

I decided now was as good a time as any to stop trying to shape myself to fit a corporate mindset. It was time to create a business for myself. I knew I was motivated, I had connections and the skills people needed. But I was nervous about gambling my lifestyle on it. I still wanted some level of security, something I could fall back on. I was adamant I couldn't lose all of the material success I had worked so hard to collect. It was the only sign of everything I'd gone through, everything I had achieved.

I believed if I worked for myself, then I would never have to go through the corporate nightmare again. I wanted something where I made the decisions, where I made the critical calls, where I could decide where my energies should be focused. But I was about to learn that this sort of freedom, if taken via the 'safe' route always comes at a cost. I was about to learn if I wasn't prepared to leap into complete independence, I'll still have to deal with arseholes.

# CHAPTER EIGHT
*How to make mistakes*

Within a few days, I touched base with an old acquaintance, a partner in a distribution company I'd done business with for years. I called to tell him of the demise of the brand I was working for. Whilst he already had a team of salespeople, there seemed to be a lack of experience and expertise in targeting or understanding major retail. I saw an immediate opportunity for us to do business together.

I presented him with an idea for a unique partnership. We went back and forth for many weeks, designing and redesigning the structure, until desperation began to set in. Remembering the dejection of redundancy, I pushed on, picturing the freedom and control I'd always wanted, almost within my reach. But by the time we reached a plausible agreement, my pay-out had all but run out, and I found myself leveraged into a corner.

What had seemed like an initial bullseye, I quickly discovered was the wrong target and I would be trying to yank the arrow free for the next couple of years. From last minute price adjustments to product catastrophes and other retail deal-breakers, one disaster led to another. There was no transparency, no flexibility and certainly no ability to listen. And it didn't matter how smart, experienced or patient I was. Neck deep in denial, I persevered without truly knowing what I was getting myself into. I may have gained a partner, an investor of sorts, but I soon realised my choice was way off.

I was working for myself now but not really. It was a 'Claytons' independence; the business you start when you're too scared to start a business.

Had I known all of this in advance, I would've pursued something else, anything else, and my target would have been in a completely different stratosphere to the one my business partner was in. Instead I was to face a shameful battle as we disentangled our partnership. This wasn't anyone's fault but my own. I had made a fundamental mistake in the way I started my new career. The safe route hadn't turned out to be the best route after all and now I had to accept defeat, go back to the beginning and start everything again.

Deep down, I believed I couldn't start a business on my own. I wanted to think I could, but the 'risk' seemed too great. I needed someone else to share it with so I could feel protected.

The disappointment of my last career choice was still hanging over me. And the now defunct partnership added an extra layer that made it almost impossible to breathe.

I spent far too much time asking myself 'why' this had happened, when I really should have been exploring 'how'. My lack of self-belief had scattered my dreams in all directions and my focus was all wrong. It wasn't that someone else had done this to me. It was me that allowed my own fear of failure to erode my confidence and blur my judgement.

What was I so afraid of? I'd failed before and been so much better off for it. But this time was different. The higher I had risen in my career, the more I felt I had to lose. But I never stopped to think whether any of it really meant anything anyway. I was too caught up in the fear of losing the 'things' I thought made my life worthwhile.

I thought I was defined by my car, our large apartment, my ever-expanding list of travel destinations. Did these make me happy though? Yes. They didn't hurt. But they were never the root of actual happiness. I'd grown so attached to the lifestyle, because it was easy and I wasn't prepared to give it up, not just yet.

But staring down another failure, out on the edge, I realised the things I loved most in the world cost me practically nothing - my wife, my music and the ability to go surfing. And they had been there with me the whole time. These three things represented my love, my passion and my freedom, all of which cost nothing.

All throughout those corporate years, I'd valued the wrong things and lost touch with what made me who I was.

I'd let go of my self-belief. I'd let go of my spark, my fun-side and sadly, the love I had for my sales career. And at my lowest point, not only did I run out of cash, but I ran out of confidence.

Despite my wife's insistence, I continued to delay all the things I should have done when the redundancy first came through. I kept hanging on to the superficialities that I thought represented who I was.

In a desperate effort to maintain an expensive lifestyle, I refused to sit still for one moment. I started applying for full-time jobs, anything and everything. I felt like my only option was to find a secure corporate job, but for a while I couldn't even get an interview. People who had once knocked on my door, were suddenly full to the brim. The market was changing, and my connections started moving on.

I had painted myself into a shitty corner and I was now paying the price for it. These months of helplessness were more stressful than all my corporate days, franchise days and the failed partnership rolled into one. I was disillusioned and confused by all of it.

I was hanging on by a thread, woven only by the three things that made sense anymore. I was surfing every chance I got, I was writing and playing music and I had my wife's support and love. These things helped me get through almost a year of frustrations and unwillingness to look reality square in the face.

Then one day my accountant called out of the blue and I discovered things were going to get a lot worse. Through a mishandling of the books a few years back, I was being smacked with a huge tax bill. I teetered on the edge of absolute breakdown. I had a lifestyle I could no longer afford; I was apparently unemployable and now through a cruelly-timed filing error, the tax man wanted to suck the last breath out of me.

But instead of falling into a fit of rage, I grabbed a notebook, turned on some music and sat in a deck chair on our balcony. I felt strangely calm. Maybe I'd copped so many hits, I finally felt no more impact. Looking out across the ocean, I should have felt overwhelmed, but I suddenly felt fired into action. I began to work on a list of all the things I could do to get myself out of this mess. Once I started it was hard to switch off, I churned out a long list, there were over a hundred things I could do to earn a living again. Immediately.

At this exact moment a critical change happened within me. I suddenly stopped worrying about all the things not working out, I decided and truly believed nothing was really that bad after all. Failure. Money. Bills. Debt. Loss of lifestyle. I couldn't care less. My sanity was far more important. Despite all the drama and shit-storms, there was value in what I do, and I'd proven this over and over again.

But now, for the first time I felt I had the ability to choose how and where I applied it.

I didn't need someone else's partnership to fall back on. If I was given the choice between long-term freedom with hard failures, or a safety net that came with shackles - I decided then and there, I would always choose freedom. Every single time. If you asked me the same question just ten minutes earlier, before my accountant's bombshell, the answer would have been the opposite. The difference now was all in my mind. The large tax bill had switched on something inside me.

Despite the long list of options, I knew all I wanted to do was return to what I did best, to focus on my business, my ability and my God-given talents. This is what I had to offer and if I stayed true to it, then it was all I could do. I no longer cared what others thought. I decided to only invest in people who believed in my work.

In the short space of receiving the phone call and walking to the balcony, I was able to detach myself from my circumstances. And this one simple action provided me with unwavering clarity.

My new goal was to create a life of choice and freedom that would allow me to explore, surf, travel, experience and learn about the world.

I was ready to think differently, but for real this time.

# CHAPTER NINE
*Think like an animal*

Starting again, my business tested me beyond any of the limits I thought I had. But the true test was learning the importance of why I had to keep going no matter what. With all the failures I'd experienced to date, I'd become strangely comfortable with not getting what I wanted. But I wanted to pursue my consultancy business more than anything. Everything before it led me to this point. I had to trust my instincts and keep taking steps.

I knew I needed to be carefully hungry if I was ever going to find a way to make my business progress on my own terms, knowing if I failed, I could lose it all again. But I thought perhaps this could produce my best work. If I had only one option, then I'd be compelled to focus on the many ways and means of making it happen.

I had always believed it was smart to have a backup plan. If things didn't work out, then I could fall back on an alternative option. But when I resumed my venture alone, I began thinking that 'Plan B' was not a reliable strategy to have. I didn't want an out when things got rough or I was pushed to the brink. Limiting myself to one option took a mental toughness well beyond anything I was prepared for. And my instincts were tested with every decision.

I set about re-designing the business, its structure and its function into something I could grow on my own. It would be a business focused on what I loved to do and what I did best, valuing and never compromising my work. I wanted it to function in harmony with my lifestyle and personal ambitions. Ambitions that didn't resemble those I had mistakenly strived for before.

Letting go of past aspirations and their failure was tough, but crucial to move forward, it allowed me to find the freedom of movement in beginning again. I needed to believe in my own ability to cultivate fresh opportunities and sniff-out those leading to gut-ache. This time, there could be no more vomit-induced realisations.

I now had to be flexible and change instead of being so attached to how I would achieve the outcomes I wanted. If I was going to make my business a long-term success, I had to see the change for what it was - simply a chance to do things a different way.

I had an opportunity now to let go of the corporate lifestyle I'd been clinging so desperately to. As long as I loved what I was doing, it didn't matter if it was perfect or not. I just needed to keep moving. Things would always be in a constant state of change and I could never really know where these changes might lead.

Despite all of the upheaval in my thinking and approach to my business, I was starkly aware I felt the most common fear known to man - the fear of failure. The thought I might get it all wrong had paralysed me in the past and shadowed many of my earlier career decisions. But I could see now it never should have. No matter how bad things turned out, I always managed to find a way through it.

We should never underestimate the power fear has over our minds.

It can unwittingly control our thoughts and behaviours, influencing our personal and professional lives. We might think fear is a natural instinct that protects us from harm, but there is also a lot to be gained if we harness it to push us out of our comfort zones.

Since my early surfing days, I had one of those framed posters up on my wall, a picture of a monster wave with a surfer in the foreground, punctuated by the slogan: "Face your fears, live your dreams". I'd bought it as motivation to keep up my surfing and challenge myself to go out on bigger days, but I'd kind of missed the point. The fear that gets in the way of 'living your dreams' is not a physical threat. It's psychological fear that does the most damage.

As I faced going it alone in business, for what I hoped was the first and only time, I recognised fear was simply there to force the smartest and most instinctual choices. I couldn't just face fear to create the life I wanted, I had to learn how to embrace it and bring it along for the ride.

There were two moments over the next few months that brought it all home and filled me with a huge sense of ownership and pride. The first was receiving notification of share transfer, finally becoming one hundred percent owner of the company I had started. I was free now to do what I wanted with the business I aspired to begin; I was free of suffocating partnerships.

The second, was to change the name of the company to the one I wanted but had been talked out of: Taco Stand. I chose the name 'Taco Stand', not only because of my love of Mexican food, but because of the energy I felt the words encapsulated. "Let's blow this Taco Stand!" sounded more than appropriate for my circumstances, it was my search for something better.

Taco Stand could take the form of anything I wanted it to be. It gave me the freedom to design the business my way.

Conveniently, the name 'Taco Stand' also acted as a filtering mechanism for potential clients. Anyone who asked about the name negatively, would identify themselves as someone who wasn't open to doing things differently. Perhaps they wanted to but weren't really ready. Those who liked it however, seemed to love it and remembered me and what I stood for - I was challenging the way things were done and accentuating the importance of standing out from everyone else.

When confirmation came through of the name change, I finally felt like my own man. I left behind the toxic partnership, along with a pile of old business cards which I unceremoniously dumped in the trash.

Within months I narrowed in on two potential brands based out of China and was heading off to Shenzhen to meet with the owners and tour their factories. My inaugural international trip as the solo Taco Stand director passed by in a blur of overwhelming Chinese hospitality. Between four-hour presentations and food that blew the taste buds off our tongues, we had a blast. The sense of fulfilment I gained when both brands agreed to my representation was a feeling I'll never forget. This was real now. These were opportunities that otherwise didn't exist. I was creating something for myself from nothing, with only my efforts going in and only myself to blame if things didn't work out.

Nothing can prepare you for the extreme learning curve when starting your own company. It's not just the highs that are higher, the lows hurt and stay with you, scars on the heart of what keeps you pumping. I found my balance - I take full responsibility, I have the power to make all the decisions, but I take all the hits and body blows along the way. And the bonus? Every little decision has a net-effect, which sharpens your skills in the most unexpected ways. I had no major company to cheer me on or guarantee my salary, just myself and a ton of self-belief.

I was now functioning in a world of constant progression, I had no choice but to improve, to grow, to get better at what I was trying to do. I had to create every opportunity, knowing if I didn't make the sale or ship a product, then I wouldn't make any money. This was my new reality. It made me hungry, really hungry. I couldn't be complacent or ignore problems, every department of Taco Stand was my department.

I was really surprised by the deep sense of satisfaction and happiness that came with building something for myself. I always wondered why my wife got a kick out of making her own clothes, but in a funny way I began to really get it. Seeing your efforts grow from raw materials into something tangible made me feel completely fulfilled. The moments when I surprised myself with the reception of a presentation or the achievement of a sale, was all the validation I needed. It ingrained in my psyche that I was in fact meant to do this.

The more I began to love building my own business, the more it became a part of me. I started to see the world differently. The freedom to do things the way I thought they should be done and the freedom to pursue the products and business relationships I thought would be valuable, this is where I started to create my best and most gratifying work.

In hindsight, my desire for career freedom had been something I'd ignored for years. But the longer I ignored this desire, the harder my professional and personal life became. I could now change all of this.

When I started Taco Stand, I chose to never put myself in that vulnerable position again. How I run my business, was limited only by my imagination. And this freedom enabled me to develop a lasting peace of mind, which sticks with me today.

As the dots finally connected, I had more time to surf and enjoy life again, even if I didn't have the money to go on exotic surf trips. It didn't matter.

I no longer felt like I was fighting against the large organisations that once had me feeling so caged. Instead I began to work with them and could now see the value in their structures, even if it wasn't a perfect machine. I could work alongside them, without being involved in the politics, policies and procedures. All the brutal corporate experiences I'd collected in the past gave me intimate insights into how I could better fill the gap for brands who needed someone exactly like me. All of this provided greater strength and purpose to my business. The source of so much past frustration would give me an advantage that I could pass on as a niche service only I was able to perform.

My work was no longer my work. Taco Stand became a passionate part of my life that I loved. It was my art, my authentic expression of creativity and my hunger for more.

# CHAPTER TEN
*What Hustle taught me....*

Everyone's experience of life is different.

You're not me and I'm not you. It is our stories, our experiences and our unique perspectives that make us who we are. Our biggest frustrations surface when we try to jam individual minds and ideas into pigeon holes and give them perfect little labels in order to define them. It is possible for people to happily thrive in this securely enclosed space. But it depends on what motivates you.

Why do you do what you do? Does this reason alone have the substance you believe it does? If it's wealth, property, freedom or success you are after, it's best to determine those things for yourself. We can no longer rely on the preconceived ideas we absorb from films, TV, books or media. We must dispose of standard thinking so we can think for ourselves.

Before Taco Stand, I was motivated by money and the promise of what I believed money would give me. I was not motivated by my passions. The painful but attractive 'safe' road was simpler to follow back then, as many others were doing it right there before me.

Doing what you love can be extremely hard and comes at a heavy cost. But it is worth the price of entry. All the battles, the criticism and all the self-doubt were rolled into one neat little ticket - I had arrived. Following my heart and my instincts, I found myself standing outside the expected 'norms'. This was where I could create my own labels, I could define myself as I wished.

Hustle taught me to always explore my limits, to be curious, to test and to challenge. Nothing is forever, jobs come, and careers go. Our failures hold tremendous value and our fears are not there to be feared. Staying true to what you believe and having faith in the work you do, is all that really matters.

My years of Hustle provided me with tangible, flexible assets, ones I could take into my professional and personal life. But the start of Taco Stand was just the beginning. I was soon to experience the world of solo business within some of the hardest lessons. But I was clearly on my way to turning life from a relentless Hustle, into the ultimate nirvana of endless Froth.

PART TWO
# FROTH

Froth:
"to bubble energetically"
"to agitate in liquid"

Who knows where I'd be today if I didn't surf.

What started out as pure curiosity and an antidote to stress, became a life-changing source of inspiration.

In the beginning, I only knew that surfing was fun, which was enough for me. It wasn't until I looked a little closer, I noticed there was a whole world of other benefits. Layer upon layer, I could relate so many aspects found in surfing to my approach to life and even to business. It had entered my life with perfect timing, just when I was looking for anything to distract me from the chaotic madness. Surfing put me somewhere else.

I always felt a strong attraction to the ocean, despite (or maybe because I was) living in a land-locked city. From the books I read to the shows I loved to watch, explorers like Jacques Cousteau and the stories of "20,000 Leagues Under the Sea" captured my often-scattered attention and engulfed me in their wonder. When I was very young, I would draw elaborate pictures of underwater scenes, with sharks attacking divers and their boats. Growing up far from the ocean only increased my interest in this alien world.

Summer holidays were treasured opportunities to explore my infatuation. In my teens I started skin diving, every chance I could get.

Chucking sickies to drive the hazardous two hours, to spend a few hours in the ocean. My efforts were always rewarded. On one occasion, within minutes of submersing, I found myself surrounded by a fever of large rays. I froze and watched with awe, as they glided majestically aside, above and below me, covering the entire sea bed.

Surfing was like nothing else in my life. And the sense of continuous discovery was just another part of the attraction to it. Nothing calmed me quite like paddling out on my board. It didn't matter that I was learning in my twenties, the feeling of being out in open ocean was enough to know there was more to it than just catching a wave. And so, started an ongoing journey, as surfing would be the one constant in my life.

Over the years, surfing became more than an escape, more than a release. It's a continuous motivator, providing me with the tools to help me navigate through some of my most extreme challenges by blocking out all the noise from the world around me, and bringing everything back into focus - mind, body and nature.

When I was surfing, I felt I had a home, a place to centre myself, gather my thoughts and breathe. It's the perfect distraction. The world of schedules and deadlines were replaced with no particular place to go. Just me, my board and the ocean.

The more I surfed, the more I was drawn to its authenticity and rawness, from brutal power to peace and tranquillity. It didn't matter what sort of day I had or where my head was at, the ocean's energy never discriminated. Happy, sad, rich or poor - every single living thing is the same to the ocean. It is a balancing force, that strips you back. It is not interested in your stories, your salary, or your ego, the ocean is totally neutral and un-impressible. It doesn't reward bravado or wealth - it demands connection and respect.

Many of my best experiences have come through surfing. But

beyond the thrills and excitement, surfing simply changed my life. It changed my perspective, my mindset and my approach. The surfing lifestyle is as rewarding, as it is deep. But the act of surfing itself, is just the beginning. It's not just the physical and mental benefits of surfing I get so much from, surfing somehow makes me better at everything I do.

Other than the extremely talented and select few, the vast majority of surfers don't surf for money. We surf because we love it. "I hate surfing", said no surfer, ever. We may, from time to time whinge about the conditions, the crowds or the lack of waves, but deep down we're still in love with the one activity we devote our free time to.

Surfing not only makes me happy, it also gives me a shot of confidence and enables balance in my life. When I experience this sense of balance, my mind is calm, relaxed and more open to what life throws at me. Surprisingly, it also helped me reassess the real 'worth' of what I value in life.

No one can buy the joy surfers experience when in the water. It was, however, possible to put a price on all the things I purchased to help replicate that same joy when I was on dry land. As I re-evaluated the things that made me happy, I questioned the value I attached to time, material possessions, relationships and other priorities. And surfing helped me put it all into perspective.

Surfing became my daily meditation. And like learning meditation, there was no short cuts, there was no cut and paste. I could only apply time, effort and patience. Throughout each progression, frustration and break-through, I never stopped searching for the ultimate feeling of completely switching off from the rest of the world.

Surfing may look like a series of actions and techniques, but this is just a small part of the picture. Despite being complex and challenging to pick up, the physical skills can only take you so far. Great surfers possess more than just the practiced motor skills, they hold an inner instinct, a deep understanding and connection to the ocean. The surfer's most expressive art is on display when they embody this connection and allow themselves to effortlessly flow with the ocean's energy.

The hidden gift in the experience of surfing is the opportunity to relax and breathe as you focus only on the present. There is only one thing that travels through a surfer's mind when on a wave - it's a single moment of all-encompassing connection and the complete absence of everything else. It's an addiction to this very feeling that draws a surfer to the ocean. This alone has the power to change a person and the way they live. It goes far beyond motivation or inspiration.

While focusing on the pure pleasure of surfing helped to pull me through the challenging and difficult times, it was the unexpected benefit of finding connection within myself that would inspire me to take action. As my connection through surfing deepened, it unlocked something inside me and changed my approach to not only my personal life, but my business too.

And this is how I found myself at the point where the Hustle within my mind began to dissolve and I was able to make significant changes that facilitated the evolution of what I would come to call the surfer's mindset.

# CHAPTER ELEVEN
*The Stoke cures all*

My first year of business was a serious wake up call. Doing it alone was no walk in the park and at times no amount of instinct or expertise could help me breakthrough in an industry with tightening models and preference for house-brands. I worked hard, but the consumer industry was buckling-down around me. No one was buying what I had for sale.

Countless publishing house tours, sales presentations and trade shows resulted in little more than increased exposure for the global brands I represented. However, with every journalist, product manager and category buyer I met, my pitch became more refined, my passion grew stronger and my belief in what I was doing strengthened.

I spoke with more distributors, brands and manufacturers looking for opportunities, but with each pivot in my plan of attack, I was faced with resistance. It didn't matter what I wanted or how strong these opportunities were; I was trying to alter how business was done in an industry where the dinosaurs still ruled.

The time came to admit that I had to approach things in a completely different way. Relying solely on my business to earn an income while I was still building its foundations was not working out. But I was determined to not reach for the employment advertisements just yet. I had to find another way to keep a roof over our heads, while keeping my dream alive. And my love of surfing helped me to do just that.

What should have been some of the most soul-destroying rejections and setbacks, were now easier to survive because of the daily routine I allowed myself to settle into. And so, my most urgent priority of every morning, was the surf.

I don't know why I bought my first surf magazine at age nineteen. We lived hours from the beach, where there was nothing even resembling a surf culture. Yet, I was drawn to the bright blue cover and adventurous spirit encased in the glossy pages, their description of the 'surfing lifestyle' seemed so other-worldly. Visually it looked stunning, the pages were full of pristine beaches, perfect waves, bikini-clad girls, dudes with sun-bleached hair and faces painted in zinc cream like tribal warriors.

The original 'Point Break' film had just been released and the character 'Bodhi' was the subject of an article about his search for spiritual essence. 'Bodhi's' philosophy of life was that everything moved in a circular fashion and due to his connection to the ocean, he too chose to live by the cycles of nature. For 'Bodhi', surfing was a state of mind - a place to both lose yourself and find yourself. Corny as it was, it got my attention.

This was completely at odds with everything I'd mistakenly associated with surfing to date. Surf-fashion hadn't hit the mainstream yet and surfers were largely portrayed by Hollywood as hippies and dole bludgers, with the kitsch of sixties teen-surfing films a distant memory. Typical images of surfing fed to the world in the eighties were 'Spicoli', rolling out of a smoke-filled van in 'Fast Times at Ridgemont High'. Everything was 'rad', and surfers seemed to get a bad reputation in response.

But my impression of it changed when I learnt about the surfer's spiritual connection to the ocean, even if it was through a character in a blockbuster film. The article made surfing sound like a noble passion, one that people looking for more from life might be driven to pursue, not a slacker pastime.

On any given morning in Sydney, you were more likely to see a surfer getting out of a BMW than rolling out of a smoke-filled van. But despite the sport's progression, popularity and acceptance in the twenty-first century, there are many people who still look at the surfing lifestyle and scratch their heads. And there's a good reason for this. Surfers *are* different. It's not because of their jargon or how they look, the real difference is on the inside. This is due to the fact a surfer's obsession teaches them how to think differently.

And it comes down to the 'stoke'.

The only way to describe the almost indescribable feeling surfers experience when catching a wave, is it's an all-consuming state of euphoria - pure happiness, presence and excitement. Often compared to flying, it can feel like a surreal weightlessness with the power to suspend time, a sensation of freedom, joy and adventure, all rolled into one. Those who surf are generally aware of this feeling and the positive influence it can have on other parts of their lives. It's the reason we go back for more and get grouchy when we go without.

Nothing beats the rush, the absence of the world around you and the feeling of being one with the wave. Riding the ocean's power, even for just one fleeting moment, is unforgettable and addictive. Yet, if the stoke is harnessed not just as a momentary thrill, but as an energy source to be applied to life, then its benefits can extend well beyond the physical.

As I settled into a daily routine of morning surf sessions, no matter what the conditions, my confidence as a surfer grew. I also found I was able to transfer the stoke in a pretty potent way to manage the extreme stress I was under in the first year of business. Prioritising my physical, mental and, in a way, spiritual health every day enabled me to handle the frequent disappointments and view them as part of the cycle of life. No matter what lows I might reach throughout the day, I knew there would always be the high waiting for me in morning.

The stoke was a natural extension of my love for surfing, it instinctively supported me to go with the flow of life's journey. It was the first thing that helped me see everything from a nature-based and evolutionary perspective. And although I had to face some hard truths about the life I'd been living, it made it so much easier to change the way I was viewing the world.

# CHAPTER TWELVE

*Nature is the only reality*

During this stressful time, I desperately clung to the Northern Beaches lifestyle I'd worked so hard to achieve. I didn't want to let go of my ocean views and afternoon sea breezes, which provided so much relief from the chaos of my working life. When every morning approached, I'd grab my surfboard and run across the road and all the fear of escalating rent and lifestyle costs would momentarily disappear, like someone else's problem.

It was during this daily surf routine, I became friends with an older neighbour. We would bump into each other most mornings, his apartment block across from ours, but his balcony opening right onto the sand of our local beach. I'd hear this strange throaty call - "Errr", coming from the balcony of his top-floor apartment as he caught me surveying the surf conditions. It didn't take long for a friendship between us to form as our chats became a regular feature of the day.

Our neighbour owned a tidy gardening business. From my office desk I could see him packing up the truck and trailer before heading off to spend his day outdoors. It was the complete opposite of my day, which had me barely clinging to sanity, desperately seeking a solution amongst a fresh batch of uninspiring email responses.

When we saw each other, he complained about his body-soreness and me about my business stresses. I was growing increasingly envious of the format of his work, there seemed to be a genuine honesty to it, with no politics or unreasonable external forces. He also enjoyed the additional perk of starting and finishing a project in the same day, whereas I had just found myself spending twelve months on a brand I'd gained nothing but frustration for the time invested. His work seemed to be a simple and authentic way to make money - with the bonus of being outdoors, surrounded by nature.

It was during one of our morning chats, when our neighbour offered me a few days' work in the garden for some extra income. At this point I just wanted to earn some money to help me shake the desperation. I was also looking forward to spending a day in another world, a world that would hopefully treat me kindly. I knew nothing about gardening other than very occasionally mowing the lawn as a kid. And I hadn't done any real physical work since the milk-run in high school. But I was looking forward to it. I was looking forward to just being a body on a job for a few days, with no pressure on my mind.

My first day gardening started with three of us squeezing into the front seat of my neighbour's truck, the smell of sunscreen and fresh fertiliser filling the cabin as eighties rock distorted its way through the speakers. We arrived at a huge property on Sydney's North Shore, a house reminiscent of old English cottages complete with long manicured hedges and lush garden beds.

After we spilled out of the truck, my neighbour handed me a rake and pointed me in the direction of the driveway. In my excitement, I went hard and fast, and within ten minutes I'd accumulated two giant blisters. Looking down at my pulsating hands, I knew it was going to be a long and physical day.

I hadn't felt this kind of pain and exhaustion before and I was surprised it felt so good to be working in the dirt, sweat drenching my shirt and soil lodged under my nails. When we finished and packed everything back into the truck, it was with a great sense of satisfaction, a feeling that had eluded me over recent months. To do the work and see the immediate transformation was gratifying, and being outside in nature was extremely cathartic.

That first night I slept better than I had in a long time. Instead of tossing and turning worrying about the future, I laid there in a coma-like state for a solid eight hours. I woke to a pocket of cash and a new found respect for my neighbour's working life.

The effort I'd put in was duly rewarded and over the coming months I was able to pick up as much gardening work as I wanted. The more I sweat and the more exhausted I felt, the more I came to enjoy this way of life. Surf in the morning, gardening all day. I was miles from the sales floor, meeting rooms and my laptop. It proved to be the perfect disconnection and mental detox.

I still had plenty of 'beans on the boil' with Taco Stand, but it was no longer my hourly focus or detention. The more I detached from the day-to-day business desperation, the more I could focus on the passion and love for what I was working on. Its existence was the real reason behind me gardening in the first place. It might have started as a simple way to make money but in its own strange way, gardening created the support system I never knew I needed.

Somehow the two work responsibilities harmonised and complimented each other. Gardening, like surfing, had a grounding effect on me. I was able to work physically during the day and apply myself mentally to grow my business from late afternoon and into the night. There was no longer any pressure to make Taco Stand a roaring overnight success, I could simply be grateful for the luxury to do it the way I wanted.

For the first few weeks, I wore every callous like a badge of honour. It made me laugh to think about just how delicate and self-absorbed my previous corporate life was. I was now doing business in a way I'd never considered before, and it was turning out to be extremely effective.

I find it difficult to explain to an office-bound worker just how good it feels to be working outside with your hands, producing something you can surround yourself in. Back in my suit wearing days, I would have been sitting down for lunch, looking at the workers in their muddy boots, thinking to myself, "No way". The comfort of being behind a desk can seem like the better alternative, until you actually experience the freedom of being out in the garden. Now I found myself to be the one in the gardening gear, covered in dirt, looking at the guys in suits and thinking to myself, "No way, man. No way". When I settled into my new work, I realised I wouldn't have it any other way.

Gardening and spending time absorbed in nature put me back on track financially and mentally. I was learning from all my failed experiences and investing the knowledge back into my business. I was working and living more authentically, more honestly. I was being true to my own goals and intentions and it felt great.

Gardening gave me options. I felt free, no longer trapped by the limitations of my chosen field and circumstances. We weren't living a life of luxury, but it all depends on how you define 'luxury'. At that time, I could derive extreme pleasure simply from a glass of ice water during the day, the ability to surf when I wanted and the opportunity to detach from my world of frustration. It was a luxury to come home each afternoon and work to build my business, with a renewed focus and zero compromise.

Gardening was bloody hard work and although it was never going to make me rich financially, it didn't need to. What it did for me mentally, for my lifestyle and for my health were where its true riches lay. I was experiencing and exploring a side of myself I didn't know existed.

The one constant at the centre of this personal transformation was the gentle existence of nature. I was no longer oblivious to its simple beauty. The smell of fresh mulch, the contrasting colours, the explosive bursts of flowers and the cool stillness in winter. How much of this I'd completely ignored on the pathway to more. These simple pleasures reinforced what made life worth living, and it was not the accumulation of corporate 'success'.

Despite how the vast majority of urbanites and corporates live today, history demonstrates that the human body was designed for physical movement, not to sit stationary behind a desk or in front of a screen.

After working long days in the garden, I am convinced of the endless benefits of spending a period of your life working in an outdoors environment, for two main reasons. One is to simply have the opportunity to learn from and develop an understanding and appreciation of nature. The second is to recognise the true value in physical work, to learn it's not what you get for it but how you value what you get for it.

Our digital-driven society underrates the importance of connecting to the earth, but it is a source of respite for all of humankind, it's part of us, it's in our DNA.

Work pressures, consumer debt, growing landfill, severe weather, all cause me to worry about the increasing number of people who are deprived of regular connection to nature and how this affects their respect for our natural environment. What's going to happen if these people are one day responsible for protecting the very environment they are disconnected from?

During my most financially successful and stressful years, I had drifted off course. Before I knew it, I was deep into an empty space, one I tried to fill with attachment to possessions and a freakish desire to control everything. I had created a world at the mercy and reliance of external forces. I was trapped and fearful of change. But gardening, physical work and my new appreciation for nature brought me back down to earth and out of my head. It reminded me of my size and place. Simple as that.

And now I had the chance to inject these learned values where they could really make a difference for me long-term - into Taco Stand.

Wouldn't it be great if everyone could experience the feeling surfer's experience - without fear and without all of the other things that prevent people from trying something new?

It's a curious proposition, an interesting thought experiment. How different would the world be if everyone on earth connected to nature and experienced the peace and euphoria surfers do? Would this make the world a better place?

What if everyone surfed? It would likely crowd out every local break, we can bet on this, but would the West's obsession with buying alternative joy be the same? Would everyone become more centred and in touch with what really matters? What would become of the greedy? Would they still value the same empty 'things'? Or would they become impervious to the marketing machine that 'carrots' their attention? What would become of our priorities, would nature take precedence, or would we still be enamoured by our possessions?

Would people start to see how crucial our planet is to our survival? And not just for the resources we thoughtlessly strip from it? If we recognise just how little we need to make us happy, would we stop trashing the planet with our throw-away lifestyles? Are we here to steal from it, rape and pillage, or are we supposed to learn from it?

What else can we gain from nature's view? Can we put an end to racism, sexism and inequality? Could it actually bring people together in a common understanding of what is really important? Will it enable us to re-evaluate how we live and reprioritise how we spend our time? Would we then open our arms to those in need?

This may be a little extreme but the possibilities of a world filled with people who have a nature-focused, surfer's mindset is something I've wondered about. In the Western world, we have a tendency to place a value on the unnecessary and devalue the things not sold to us. Consumer possessions, material success, these things may have value in a commercial or temporary sense, but they amount to nothing when you are dust in a casket. They are an empty pursuit and a distraction from living, at best.

We go from house to garage and drive our cars to work, where we park underground and catch the lift until we arrive at a desk - modern city lifestyles encourage avoidance of, rather than connection to, the earth. The very thing responsible for us existing in the first place. We forget it's the planet who owns us, not the other way around. I can see why some people may have a sense of entitlement. But whatever you believe, it's hard to ignore that we are in deep shit with Mother Nature.

I'm not suggesting we all toss in our careers to plant our feet in the dirt or take off on a surfing sabbatical. But I guarantee anytime spent in focused contemplation of nature, could start the process toward deeper thoughts on life. This only hit me when I started surfing, and it especially hit me when I started working in the garden. My newly inspired connection to nature changed my whole perspective on life, work and money. Things I once walked past in a phone-screen-haze, emails and rush to get somewhere else, now captured my attention and admiration. There's so much to gain from a quiet moment in nature. From the second I started working as a gardener I was fascinated by all aspects of it, but it is surfing and the total immersion and synchronicity of the ocean, which holds the ultimate connection with life.

# CHAPTER THIRTEEN
*View the world from a new perspective*

It wasn't long before I wanted to be more than a 'body-on-a-job'. Never one to settle for being at the bottom of even an unspoken hierarchy, I decided to take the potential for income from gardening more seriously.

I picked up some extra days work with a local landscaper. We had met through our shared coffee and surf spots, becoming great mates over the years and every time I put on the boots to be a part of his team, I'd learn something valuable. Over days of training, fat-Friday lunches and Chiko Rolls, his encouragement soon inspired me to launch out as a gardener on my own. A decision that would give me even more freedom and money to support the longer-term goals of Taco Stand.

Starting my own gardening business was about taking a chance on something unexpected. I had no idea where it would lead or even how long I could sustain doing it. This was a completely new approach for me in a professional sense. At times, I didn't know if this road would take me further from Taco Stand, or if I'd stumbled across a convenient short cut. Either way, I'd taken a wildly unexpected turn.

Many mates helped get my new endeavour up and running, sending jobs, loaning tools and giving plenty of advice. They helped me build the independence to create a stable and fun little business. But it wasn't just the work they sent me that I'm eternally grateful for, it was the ripple effect the gardening work had on my company that really made a difference. My friends' support enabled me to not only build a new source of income, it allowed me to re-build Taco Stand exactly how I wanted to, on my own terms.

A year into gardening and I bought an old ute, had collected a handful of tools and left some business cards down at my local cafe. I loved driving that old ute, it had a beautifully restored blue vinyl interior, aptly named 'Toyota Grinner'. It was bursting with personality and I had zero regrets switching from the extravagant car that had become a noose around my neck.

Gardening during the day gave me the head space to come up with new approaches for tackling challenges in Taco Stand, while my sales experience from the corporate world helped me build a sustainable gardening business with a constant flow of new referrals. Doing something that contrasted significantly with my professional work, meant neither business dominated my life nor dictated what I did. I chose to look at my unusual circumstances from a positive perspective so I could always use it to my advantage, instead of thinking about the possible negatives of my situation.

As soon as I felt back in control, my stress reduced dramatically and I genuinely felt happier, it was purely an awareness of mindset.

I didn't feel pushed into anything, there was no one telling me what to do and I was creating everything I wanted, how I wanted. As my gardening business grew, so too did my fascination with nature. I set about studying as much as I could about all facets of the work, from plant types and names, to construction and garden design. I'd seen and heard enough to get a good handle on what customers expected and needed from a gardener, so I set about giving them exactly this.

My plan was simple, to create a small business that over-delivered in its promise and focused on customer service and people skills - two things I knew by heart. Soon my schedule was completely filled. It happened so quickly. All of my most loyal clients came from word of mouth, friends and neighbours of the people who already valued the work I did.

Somehow, I'd discovered the perfect recipe. I had the freedom to choose what needed to be done and a working lifestyle with the flexibility to put my energy where it was needed most. Some days I was mowing a lawn five minutes from home, while others were a solid eight hours rolling out new turf. It gave me time to deliver on my new vision for earning an income while still feeling a sense of achievement at the end of every day. The choice to garden as my main financial source wasn't a cop out, it wasn't a distraction or act of desperation, it was a choice that empowered me. And in the process, it gave Taco Stand every chance of success.

I learned the power of perspective from a friend who helped me manage my stress during the hardest period of my corporate life. She had me imagine all of my worries and sources of anger and stress as a massive ball weighing heavily in my arms. Next, I would imagine the ball shrinking down to the size of a pea, that neatly fit in the palm of my hand, easy to manage, easy to control. It sounded impossible at first, but when I mastered it, it was a major shift. It made me see the power of choosing the perspective from which I viewed things in life. My problems were always much smaller than me.

Gardening and surfing also helped me do exactly this. They put a distance between me and my financial fears, the stress and the busyness of running two competing businesses.

This wasn't the first time I experienced the importance of 'perspective', but it was definitely when I had to stretch the theory to absolute extremes to gain the most out of it. At the time I could've seen gardening as my only choice and the only way to earn money going forward or I could have believed I had to apply for corporate jobs, give up on Taco Stand and have the security of money in the bank again. But instead of thinking I had to choose just one way forward, which can be how life looks when you are facing huge challenges, I realised that perspective also enables you to look at life in a totally new way. In reality we don't have one way to do things, we have a kaleidoscope of choices.

If I hadn't been open to the possibilities, I doubt I would have made it, not with my sanity anyway. Looking through a kaleidoscope at the life before me, provided many alternative pathways, but still with the end goal very much in view.

I found it was possible to see opportunities in just about anything, whether it was the random choice to go gardening for a day or to pull beers back at the pub. The key was to be open - and to never expect a straight line to your desired destination. I was prepared to deviate from the plan and take some wrong turns, yet every turn seemed to land me exactly where I needed to be.

It may sound counterintuitive and it's definitely different from what I was taught, but when I put all my energy into one way to do things, I dramatically narrowed my chances for success. When following a strict method that doesn't work out, the frustration only makes it harder to know what to do next. Putting blinkers on might cut out distractions, but it also cuts out all the opportunities for unexpected results. The end goal is better viewed as a jumbled image at the end of a kaleidoscope, with many pathways, options and choices. Taking a kaleidoscopic view of the way forward opens opportunities everyone else is blind to.

My end goal was for Taco Stand to be my sole business, but the fact was, it operated so much better because I was doing something completely different to achieve it. Taking the pressure off earning money from it, provided me with two important things - purpose and function. Not only did it operate better, the time away enabled me to see it for what it truly was. It couldn't be the source of my passion for sales; it had to be an expression of my passion for sales.

# CHAPTER FOURTEEN
*It's not what you do, it's how you do it*

And so, I began one of the busiest periods of my adult life. Most weeks I was gardening five, sometimes six days, backing it up with hours on the phone or computer at night and first thing in the morning, before I hit the beach for a welcome reprieve in the surf. The ocean rarely demanded anything of me, it was the one place I could go and not think about any of the things I had to do, at least for an hour before the rising sun told me I had appointments to make and customers to call. There was a clarity amongst the chaos.

I should have collapsed from exhaustion, or maybe thrown away at least one of the many commitments I had to follow through on, but I wasn't raised that way. My Dad taught me, "if you're going to do something, do it properly", the tired but true tale all of us have heard at some point. It became a mantra of hopeful perfectionism motivating me to care about what I was doing, even when it was something out of the ordinary, something that may be temporary, or something I just might fail at.

When I was five, Dad would frequently take me to the park to kick the footy. At the time I was happy enough to just make contact with the ball. I was just playing for fun, but Dad always insisted I had to kick the ball the correct way. It seemed so much harder to use the proper technique, it felt awkward and unnatural, and I could barely kick half the distance, but Dad insisted.

At age five, the payoff for practising technique didn't come quickly, but it did come later when I eventually put on a jersey. All the time invested in learning how to do it correctly, gave me a huge advantage over other players. I was not only punting the right way, but the ball was travelling much further than anyone else in our team (as documented in my treasured football yearbooks). It was something I became known for. When I'd get possession of the ball, parents and the coaching team would yell from the sidelines, "torpedo Browny!" and I'd kick the ball with a precision and distance I was proud of, especially at such a young age.

Precision and technique became valuable practises. I discovered my best work was often produced out of the challenges and discomfort of putting in one hundred percent. It wasn't about how much confidence I brought on the day, it was about how much effort I put in behind the scenes to ground this confidence - how much practise or research I did in my own time.

Despite competing demands, I could not afford to simply turn up and do a job. For the integrity of my gardening business, I had to research and explore all of the best options for a client's garden. And for the integrity of what I was trying to achieve with Taco Stand, I had to thoroughly prepare for every meeting, phone call or pitch email, so no one could fault the service I offered. I had to stay focused and motivated to take pride in every aspect of my work and to apply the right attitude from the first moment each new client or business opportunity arose.

When I started gardening on my own, I was determined to be really good at the skills needed to be successful. I had to take it seriously because I had no idea where this small business could lead me or what I might achieve in the process. I simply repurposed what I learned from the sales floor, be kind and be honest. I knew if I was one of the more detailed gardeners in my region, then I would likely be in demand. This strategy helped me build a tidy and profitable business.

I didn't know when I was young that being good with people would make me a successful salesman. And I didn't know when I worked hard at sales it would result in me being an in-demand gardener. Looking back, at every point of my life when I put in the effort to really care about something, it unwittingly advanced opportunities in other areas too.

Although I might have made it sound like gardening is one of life's endless joys, no one really wants to shovel five metres of soil in scorching summer sun. But when you really care about the results you want to achieve, then you take a totally different approach to the five metres. Somehow, I instinctively knew this.

It didn't matter what I was doing, what really mattered was how I chose to do it. I wasn't shovelling dirt; I was creating a new garden bed for a valued client. My motivation was to look for the art in everything I had to do, to master the technique of how it was always done and then to see if there was a more effective way to do it. I took ownership of everything, to make it something I could be proud of, to make it mine.

It was shortly after my forty-first birthday I decided it was time to apply the idea of giving one hundred percent, to my life choices. My finances, despite the extra boost from gardening, were in desperate need of resuscitation. I had to face some hard truths about what I was hanging on to, when the time had well and truly passed for me to let go.

I have always believed life is about balance, the yin and the yang, equal and opposite worlds balancing each other in an infinite perfection. But this was far from true. I was working harder and smarter than ever before, but it still didn't mean I was entitled to the rich spoils of life. I wasn't reaching the corporate income anymore and even with my wife's significant increase in pay, we simply couldn't afford the now yearly increases in rent. The balance of hard work to riches were just a smoke screen, which quickly cleared as we received another lease renewal notice, but this time with a whopping twenty-percent increase, "to bring our ten-year lease into line with properties in the area."

We'd been loyal and, in my opinion, exceptionally good renters for over a decade, and this woke me up to the changing world we lived in. No longer could we afford to live where we wanted to in Sydney, all fairness was lost in a market geared toward the wealthy.

Even though I'd believed it and lived it for years, my interpretation of balance was forced to change. I needed to experience all of it, the highs, the lows and occasionally the middle. I was finding out that balance was less about equal distribution, hard work and rewards, and all about very differently weighted priorities we could only hope would eventually lead us toward longer term goals.

I've worked in and left companies who promote a 'work-life' balance. The promise that you could leave work in the office at the end of the day, that there would be adequate reward for the hard work put in and that everyone would be treated like a member of the family - always remained elusive. I've found these versions of balance were almost always at odds with reality. 'Balance' always cost a pound of flesh with a dotted-line straight to the bottom-line. Demonstrations of commitment, sacrifice and loyalty were never balanced by understanding, care and compassion when business got tough. And this became even more prevalent when I worked for myself. Balance just doesn't exist. It is not yin and yang, it's not black and white, it's more like a jumbled mess of grey.

So, while I faced some tough realities about my life in Sydney, it became apparent there was a much bigger picture I'd lost sight of - what kind of life was I working toward and was my current life moving me closer or further away from it. My wife was right. We had to release the financial pressure to focus our money and energy in the right places, so we took our first step toward dramatic downsizing. If we were going to give one hundred percent to the life we wanted, then we had to make the hard sacrifices now.

Within a few months we found a tiny one bed, one bath apartment. We sold clothes, books, surfboards, DVDs and anything else we simply couldn't fit into our much smaller living space. It felt like a massive blow, to give up the one place that we'd made our home, within walking distance to all my favourite places. But I had to give up convenience and the feeling of home comfort to truly know what it was I was working toward - for Taco Stand to be flexible, have little restriction on what I did and no boundaries on where it could be run from.

I desired a business that could take me wherever I wanted to go or needed to go. I wanted to build something where I felt like I was making a difference and had a sense of professional fulfilment, whilst still giving me the life I wanted.

The final step in letting go of the corporate spoils from my 'previous life' meant the extravagant car had to go. We had no room for it in the garage with my increasing array of gardening tools, plus it simply didn't fit my lifestyle anymore. And as hard as it was to admit, it didn't fit me. Somewhere in my subconscious I must have thought I'd never get to own one again and perhaps this was why I'd hung onto it much longer than I really needed to. But I had to stop throwing good money after bad.

With the proceeds of the car sale, I was able to pay off its loan and upgrade the old Grinner to a ute with power-steering. The relief was unexpected. It felt so freeing to own a car outright, with no balloon or ticking time bomb hanging over my head. Soon the income I was generating through gardening was not just topping up multiple debts, we were saving towards a well-overdue holiday.

It's strange how it works, but it was around this same time, things in Taco Stand began to really come through. I started working directly with a great brand and was successful in getting them new business relationships and a steady manageable increase in sales. My hard work and tireless drive were paying off, even if just in small amounts to begin with. Balance was never about effort and reward; it was more about the whole ecosystem of life functioning together.

To the outside world, it appeared I'd taken a huge step backward. I was in a much smaller apartment, in a less desirable suburb, I replaced my crisp white shirt with a stained blue-collar, no more regular surf holidays to talk about and no new custom surf boards or fancy car to give me 'creditability'. I was no longer the corporate go-getter everyone knew me as, at least not by all obvious measures on the exterior. But making the choice to no longer keep up appearances for myself or for anyone else, was one of the most rewarding choices I've ever made. If I'd known where this new part of my journey would take me, I would have done it many years earlier.

# CHAPTER FIFTEEN
*The secret to freedom is choice*

There was a beautiful harmony and coexistence between Taco Stand, gardening and surfing. I felt fitter and happier than I'd been in a long time, possibly ever. As the months passed by, I could see how managing two businesses provided me with far greater freedom than I'd planned for. Two streams of income afforded me the luxury to be focused and very selective about how and who I worked with.

The timing was perfect for me in both businesses, especially as I was able to shape Taco Stand exactly how it would function best in the market. With the pressure of immediacy released, I focused my energies on where I could make the biggest impact. This was by working only with people who valued my work. So too with gardening, I had accumulated enough regular clients to be selective about taking on new jobs and in the end, I only worked on the projects or with the clients I would enjoy. Of course, I still had to make each project work, I still had to make money, but I was doing it on terms that would work for me into the future.

Within the space of a year, gardening on my own and taking a smarter approach to Taco Stand, my desperation had morphed into a sense of sustainable freedom. The moments of financial and professional anxiety, which would have motivated me in the past to fire off resumes for any position of slight interest, started to become a distant knee-jerk reaction.

No longer did I have the deep urge to return to the lifestyle I once believed I just 'had-to-have' to prove my worth. I was enlightened by the fact these things weren't really 'me'. Now, I was finding myself walking away from opportunities and roles that potentially could have transformed my way of life. Often it wasn't the easiest choice to make. I had several moments of self-doubt and fears of losing everything, but when I looked into the crystal ball it reflected back who I really wanted to be.

I believed more in what I was building and most importantly in the end goal of freedom and flexibility in my working life. I just knew I needed to build something for myself, no matter what.

If I hadn't started gardening, I think things would've been very different. This turned out to be the pivotal choice that completely transformed my twenty-year relationship to work and career.

Quite often it can feel like we have no choice in life. If I'm honest, this was how it felt when we downsized to a small apartment and sold my 'status' car. It felt like financially I had little choice. But in reality, this is not an accurate way of looking at the world. I did have a choice - I could've stayed in the nice apartment with higher expenses and taken a top salary job, or I could forego the luxury and earn a lot less so I could work toward building the business and life I really wanted. I had a choice and this choice gave me a sense of freedom I'd never appreciated before.

When I was in my teens, nervous about going to job interviews, an older friend told me to walk in like I've already got a million dollars in the bank. I thought it was strange advice, but I soon learned how this mindset could work in a number of ways.

Firstly, it wasn't about money. Of course, money can bring a sense of security and freedom to not worry about where your next mortgage payment, meal or bus fare will come from, but the money is simply what appears to facilitate options and choice. Secondly, money doesn't always determine your options, you do. Just as much as imagining you are wealthy gives you confidence going into a job interview, so would having two other job offers already on the table. Having options takes away the sense of fear, desperation and hopelessness.

I had created options for myself, ones only a few years before I would have scoffed at or avoided, but I now celebrated because they allowed me to approach life differently. I think it simply came down to creating my own leverage. It's something we all do unconsciously anyway, but we automatically discount our leverage and our options by thinking we have to do things a certain way. But what if you increased your awareness of all options available and gave each of them careful consideration to discover what they legitimately offer?

Leverage is not just physical, it's also psychological and it exists outside your routine thinking. It's not always obvious on the surface, you need to dig deeper and wider into all the possibilities. When you do this, you can find leverage in all things, passion, skills, even freedom, but especially in a willingness to do something completely different to what is expected.

This was how I let go of my instinct to jump back into secure corporate roles. I had to leverage my desire for flexibility and my passion for sales to find success where others didn't look. I found freedom in earning less money, in working harder and in not giving in to the pressures of what success was meant to look like.

As I found a delicate balance between gardening and pursuing my business, it dawned on me that all throughout my working years I was looking at life the wrong way. I always believed that when you left school you had to have your career figured out and know early what you were going to do for the next forty-odd years, until you earned enough money to have the life you really wanted. But when we choose career first, work becomes the focus and the basis from which everything else forms.

Our day to day lives are created by our jobs. We spend the majority of our week invested in work. From how we commute, to who we work with and the tasks that fill our day. Ultimately how you design your career is how you design your life. Money earned is just a small factor, but who really grasps this when they leave school?

For most people, chances are they get sucked into the machine and its forty-hour-week cycles. And in the worst case, many come out the other side asking, "What the hell have I been doing all my life?". Maybe we should confront a version of this question before we choose our work future, such as - "What the hell do I want to do all my life?".

Luck played a huge part in me getting the chance to explore this exact question at the mid-way point. After working toward one future for two decades, I was able to see it wasn't what I wanted. And I was incredibly grateful that when I reached the height of my corporate career, I didn't gamble my future desires on a big house and mortgage. If I had, I fear things would have turned out very differently.

Now there was space in my life, although filled with plenty of work to do, I had the opportunity to decide what I wanted my future to look like. I'd experienced the best and worst of corporate success, I had experienced the best and worst of self-employment, and I was now seeing the best and worst of the life I'd chosen in Sydney. But I had options.

I knew I wanted a life that allowed me to surf every day. I knew I wanted a life in which money wouldn't be a constant source of stress or worry. I wanted a life in which I determined for myself how and where I did my work. I wanted to travel. I wanted to be constantly inspired by new experiences, new places, new people, new challenges. And I knew staying in Sydney wouldn't give me this. The occasional overseas surf holiday or short work trip to Asia wasn't going to fulfil my desire for long-term adventure anymore.

If I continued to build Taco Stand from Sydney, with the high cost of living and constant pressures, then I could be facing many more years of gardening. Physically, I didn't think I could manage it for much longer and psychologically, I needed to escape. So, I used all the money I'd saved and booked my wife and I on an overdue six-week holiday in Bali.

This was my chance to spend some time away from Sydney, where I could measure the impact on Taco Stand when I gave it my undivided attention. My wife could also test her ability to maintain freelance clients while living in a different country. And my body could be given a chance to recoup before the hectic gardening season.

What we didn't know at the time was it would be a holiday that would determine the direction of our lives entirely.

## CHAPTER SIXTEEN
*Simple things are the best*

Bali was not on my travel radar until a surf buddy insisted I go. Before this, my opinion was based only on what I'd heard or seen on TV. I assumed it would be full of loud-mouth foreigners in Bintang singlets, wandering the streets and chugging long-necks. While it is possible to find tourists fitting this exact description in some areas, our first trip to this idyllic island taught us different.

We landed just months after the first Bali bombing in Kuta and the truth was, we hardly crossed paths with another tourist. It may have given us a sheltered first impression, but the absence of tourists gave us the opportunity to explore the entire island at our own pace. Staying in empty hotels across five different locations, we discovered much more than the negative images sensationalised back home.

I quickly fell in love with Bali. From the local food, to the humidity, the thousands of scooters and the smell of incense and flowers littering walkways, everything about it was different. True of any travel destination, Bali is what you make of it. It can either send you spare with frustration or deliver you a peaceful Zen. It depends entirely on how you choose to see the world and whether you are open to accepting this one. For me, Bali offered a rich culture based around respect and balance. And of course, it just happened to be home to some of the world's most remarkable surf.

I had returned to Bali once or twice a year, ever since our first trip well over a decade ago. And every time I learned something new. In my opinion, the 'real' Bali remains somewhat hidden thanks to the buzz surrounding the island and its hipster attractions. It is not just the persistent horn honks from passing taxis, nor is it sun lounges, umbrellas and beach hawkers interrupting your tanning session to peddle knock-off sunnies. The 'real' Bali is discovered through the Balinese people, their spiritual traditions and rich family values. And when you spend time with the locals and challenge yourself to find something different, it opens your mind to a whole other world.

After more than two years of not having the cash to leave Sydney, heading to the airport on our long-awaited holiday was possibly the most excited I'd ever been about a trip. With three surfboards and only two small duffle bags between us, I felt a sense of lightness, not just related to our lack of baggage. All of the hard work I'd done gardening and getting things just right with Taco Stand, was finally coming to fruition. I was excited for what might come, not only from surfing every day, but for what I was leaving behind.

After six weeks in Bali, everything started to look very different.

It took about a week to forget about the gardening clients I handed over to a mate back home. Another week to improve my surfing as I got into a routine of early morning expeditions. By week three we discovered more of the hidden warungs and markets we once avoided, and by the end of the fourth week, we were becoming part of the local family. Every morning, on my commute to the beach, I'd holler, "Pagi!" to our neighbours. I no longer saw it as just a holiday escape, but a research trip for our future.

And so, as we considered the fantasy of moving to Bali, we asked ourselves, what are we waiting for? Why *don't* we do this? If not now, why? When...? It seemed as if the last few years of challenges, career and life overhaul had happened to get us to this unexpected point.

I'd thought living in Sydney, having a nice home, furniture and clothing, being close to friends, shops and the beach, were a meaningful part of who I was. But as I stripped all of these things away, I honestly didn't feel like anything was missing, instead I felt like I'd gained more of myself in the process. And as I simplified my lifestyle, even if for just an experimental six-week trip, I began to feel like the fantasy was within reach.

Although our journey toward minimisation was somewhat influenced by corporate redundancy, financial hardship and a desire to work for myself - it was something I now embraced as a way of living and the essential pathway to give me the adventurous life I always wanted.

In the three years to this moment, I'd detached from the things I'd always held so tightly to and was now ready to leave in the past. But with the prospect of moving to Bali, we faced not just the minor steps of moving to a cheaper property or selling an expensive car, we now faced potentially selling everything we spent the last twelve years collecting, the symbols of my sacrifice. It felt like a momentously significant decision to make, but in all honesty, it didn't take long to see that all we had collected was 'stuff' and this 'stuff' was not life, it was just a representation of life.

# CHAPTER SEVENTEEN
*Close a window, open a door*

Thoughts of travelling the world on exciting adventures filled my dreams until my mid-twenties. It was a life I thought was way out of reach for someone like me.

But by the time I left the corporate life, I'd already been to most of the major cities I wanted to see and surfed all the local breaks while there. Despite countless mishaps, dramas and excitement - these experiences became the fond memories and funny stories I still love to tell today.

Travelling and soaking in different cultures opened my eyes to what else is out there. I'm fascinated by people and how they live in other parts of the world, their accents and their stories. Occasional language barriers were easily overcome. I always found a frequency to harmonise on, mostly through humour, laughter and fun.

Travel helped control my innate fear of missing out. I've often felt I had to satisfy a child-like curiosity I never grew out of. Perhaps the perfect place for me was somewhere else. What if I discover it in

France or Mexico? If I take a different route? What have I been missing? How could I possibly know what it is, or if it even exists, without looking? It is a temptation I find impossible to ignore.

When I hit thirty, I suddenly wanted to experience it all. And the idea of staying put for the next twenty-five years to pay off a mortgage, both terrified and bored me. I was brutally aware I might make it to the end of my days, having never found my true place. For me the choice to travel was logical.

I think the urge to explore the world is often suppressed due to responsibilities and pursuit of career. But I knew I couldn't prioritise the expectations of stability, buying a house and having a family over my desire to see the world. And I didn't want to leave it until I was retired, too old or too cranky to enjoy it. If I'm going to experience the world, I want to do it during the peak of my curiosity.

Over the years of living thick in a life of corporate 'goo', amassed in debt, my wife and I would often fantasise about a future living and working abroad. It remained a distant unachievable dream for so long, we almost gave up hope. But now we were faced with a choice, do we take the risk and move overseas, or do we settle into our life in Sydney and accept this was all there was ever gonna be?

It's not that we didn't appreciate the life we had, but we were determined not to allow our desires to dissipate into a routine or to get so comfortable we stopped challenging ourselves. We wanted to keep our romance with life alive and if we ever stayed too long, then we'd risk falling out of love with the life we were trying to build. It was time to shake off all our 'stuff' and move on.

It took just a week for 'the powers that be' to agree with us and confirm we had made the right decision. My wife found new freelance work, I picked up some big gardening jobs and we paid the deposit on a twelve-month lease in Sanur - we were now committed. We decided it was time to be light on our feet, serious about our lives and follow our dreams. Scary as that may be, we were going to make this happen.

We had only two months to get everything together and work out just how we were going to fund this new life. Properties in Bali require a full year's rent in advance, meaning we would have to pay for it not knowing what the next twelve months might bring, financially or otherwise. So, we worked our guts out for eight solid weeks. I gardened all day every day, motivated by what lay ahead. I spent my days out in the sun and dirt, and nights glued to my laptop.

As we counted down our time in Sydney, I knew I was also counting down the final days of my life as a gardener. The tidy little business of regular clients, the tools I'd collected, and my beloved ute were now for sale. I was letting go of something I had so much pride and joy in building, but I figured I could do it all again if I ever needed to.

Closing this part of my life in Australia was an unexpectedly tough thing to do. Not only were the negotiations to sell the business tedious, but the handover and saying goodbye to my clients was genuinely sad. I wasn't just giving up something that had served me well, the two years I'd spent gardening were some of the most rewarding to date. But now the space was opening up for me to focus solely on Taco Stand.

With only two weeks before we left Sydney, we madly started selling off all our belongings. It was a weird and scary process. Were we doing the right thing? Is this reversible? What if we could never afford to come back and buy all this stuff again? It was a fine balancing act to make sure we could still live in our apartment without too much discomfort, to do all the things we had to do and continue to sell off all 'non-essential' items before we set sail.

I'd always believed the point of life was to 'build' something, to 'build' towards our hopes and dreams. I believed this was done by collecting objects, establishing foundations and creating a structure around ourselves to make us who we are. However, I realised throughout this whole process that sometimes it is actually the 'tearing down' of your old life that enables the dream to take form. We'd built this life in Sydney and held on to so many things in our home and our life because they made us feel 'safe'. But this security and safety kept the status quo and kept us hanging onto a past, no longer serving us. It was this past, our past dreams and past corporate aspirations, which had been stopping us from having the freedom to travel as extensively as we'd always wanted.

Throughout my life I've always relied on my ability to visualise something to know if I was making the right choice, and anytime I struggled to get a clear picture, then perhaps it wasn't meant to be. It became a 'sixth-sense' I learned to trust. But now, every hour, day and week that passed I could feel our new life drawing closer. I could see it so clearly my excitement was almost uncontrollable.

The meagre belongings we ended up with by our final weekend in Sydney, would easily have fit into a mid-sized van. Among my cherished goods were a couple of old surfboards, guitars, vinyl records and my treasured hi-fi system. Everything else was gone. Everything else was classified 'replaceable'. All that really mattered from our life in Sydney was the things we would always carry with us - the experiences we had, the friends we'd made and the changes we made within ourselves.

Once we followed our hearts and committed to our new life our fortunes turned, even right up to the last few hours, when the final logistics of us leaving Sydney for good, fell neatly into place. A delayed flight gave us an extra moment to sit in our favourite cafe and reflect on what had been, while we dreamed of what was yet to come. It seemed at this moment, when all the sadness, fear and joy-filled anticipation came rushing in, that every little decision we'd made along the way suddenly pointed towards the life we were heading to. Every risk we had taken turned out to be the smartest choice we could have made.

Redundancies, failed endeavours, financial hardship, downsizing, starting businesses, selling businesses - everything led us to this. The adventure had finally begun. I felt a golf ball in my throat and my eyes welled, as we drove past Long Reef headland for the last time, leaving the Northern Beaches, our friends and our 'home' behind. I knew I'd miss all the people I had become close to over the last twelve years. But we now had the choice between sticking with what we knew and staying in our comfort zone or taking the first step toward freedom and adventure in the unknown. Now that we'd taken this first step, there was no going back.

# CHAPTER EIGHTEEN
*What Froth taught me*

Not everyone yearns for a tropical island life, but we all have our dream oasis. Whether it's relaxed heat, salt water and laid-back attitude you crave, or the thrill of city smells, activity and modernity, everyone has the place they want to be, the lifestyle they want to achieve.

'Froth' taught me that life is about fluidity. It's staying open to new experiences, having fun, learning and exploring. Froth requires us to test ourselves, take risks and build confidence in our abilities and instincts - to have the guts to challenge what's around us. Within it, I found the opportunity to seek what I love and the courage to forge my own path.

This was my epiphany.

While 'Hustle' provided me with the tangible hard skills and fundamental soft skills to make my way in the world, 'Froth' provided me with so much more. Surfing regularly enabled me to see my world differently, it gave me extended abilities and intangible capabilities that I could use to shape my own philosophy, my own approach to life. And it was in combining these two, in combining the skills of Froth & Hustle, I was able to turn my craft into what became my 'art'.

Frothing isn't just specific to surfing, it's a mindset to be applied to all aspects of life. As much as it's about slowing down and finding relief in nature, it's also about becoming clear about what you want, knowing what gives you the buzz and being prepared to go in a completely unexpected direction to get it. With every choice that made sense to me, there was someone removed from my immediate circle who was telling me I was crazy. But no matter how crazy things might have seemed, I had to trust there was a bigger picture I wasn't yet seeing.

Not everyone understood why I would choose gardening to earn money instead of getting a 'real' corporate job. Not everyone understood what I was trying to create with Taco Stand or how it would service a saturated market. And definitely not everyone understood why I would choose to move to Bali instead of buying a house in Sydney or having children. But the choices felt right for me and my wife, so we stuck with it and trusted it would all work out.

So, although we are now enjoying our life in Bali, the journey has only just started. We broke many 'rules' along the way, but still have more adventures we want to take. Froth & Hustle had brought me this far, but it's the combination of everything I learned in life that will take me further.

PART THREE
# THE BRIDGE

*Putting it all together*

As I sit on my pushy staring at the distant peaks out to sea, the sun breaks through the clouds over the morning horizon. Last night's cooling downpour has cleared and there is a new energy in the air.

I'm looking for signs, an indicator of what the next three hours may hold. Will I be researching, negotiating, strumming, strategising, deep in thought, on an adventure, or surfing. As the increasing light reveals the ocean's glassy surface and nearby palms swing offshore, my decision is made. Within twenty minutes I'll be immersed in the salt again.

After a few hours of play, I'll likely be sipping an iced coffee as morning commuters scooter and toot their way through the narrow streets of Sanur. This is when I'll crack open my laptop and allow all the inspiration from the morning's surf to permeate my work. Guided only by nature, with no awareness of time, no schedule to keep, these are the best days, the most productive and the most joyful. Every day holds something different and that's exactly how it should be.

Staring into the sea on these beautiful mornings puts everything into perspective. This is a rare and special experience, but it's more than this, it's an adventure, it's what I work and sacrificed for. I am so grateful for taking all those chances and for trusting my instincts. But I am especially grateful for having the courage to be honest with myself. For daring to do it on my own terms.

It is only through these terms, which took form in hindsight, that I was able to discover how I was meant to live life. We're rarely told it's okay to do things differently. But it is often only through challenging the status quo we can discover how both Froth & Hustle work together, feed each other and enable a self-designed life. It was only in burning off opinions and expectations of others that I was able to find clarity, drive and inspiration to create a life that made sense to me.

These are the terms on which Froth & Hustle exist.

# CHAPTER NINETEEN
*Term 1: Define success*

I learnt about happiness and success in the same way most kids do, through television, movies and advertising. Becoming an adult was all about the chase for work and money, and the life these things would buy me. With every pay rise, every promotion, every new opportunity, I felt more success and had more money to splash around, but I never stopped to question why I actually felt less freedom. The riches of owning more stuff, came with increased responsibility, increased debt and increased restrictions on what I could actually do with my time.

As I became aware of the unhappiness, which was part of the package deal success delivered, it became clear the success I was having wasn't made up of things that actually made me feel free or happy. What I'd built wasn't what I wanted. I had trusted in the illusions of material and career success, but for me they had proven to be empty, meaningless and soul-destroying. I'd spent the first twenty years of my career chasing success, without questioning if I was chasing the kind of success that meant something to me. But I was fortunate to see this before it was too late.

The events forming my early career, although giving me valuable experience, taught me that just because I could do something, it didn't automatically mean I should. Having goals and chasing your heart's desires are both necessary parts of life, but I was surprised to discover the goals I was working toward didn't match my own picture of what success looked like. The definition of success I pursued was all wrong.

Perhaps I'm alone in these thoughts, or maybe I failed to see this sooner than most people do. But now it seems so blatantly obvious that every individual needs to question the kind of success they may be blindly pursuing.

The things that gave me a sense of success weren't material at all. What made me feel successful was achieving freedom in my life, by seeing I had choice and the ability to create something of substance for myself. It was mental, not physical.

We're taught that success is determined by how much money we make, how big our house is, the badge on our car or the label on our clothes. This positions money as the most desirable currency, the one currency determining 'success'. But this causes us to forget about the real-life currencies such as time, freedom, love and happiness, and so we toss them out of our overall plans of achievement. But aren't these the true motivation behind the endless pursuit of money?

The only true definition of success is the one you define for yourself. When I realised this, it completely changed the goals I was working toward and gave everything I did a greater sense of purpose. I no longer desired the millionaire or wealthy lifestyle, because my values had shifted.

My life became about finding what success meant to me and it turned out to be very different to what I had been chasing for all these years. For me, success was about maximising three values: freedom, happiness and simplicity. When I began to work on creating more of the things that gave me these values, I began to feel so much more 'successful'.

I didn't get a sense of freedom, happiness and simplicity from having more money, although as my business grew it did help ease the pressure. What really gave me the feeling of success were changes that may seem inconsequential to others but meant a great deal to me. It was things like having the freedom to schedule my work around surf conditions, owning a car I bought with cash, living within walking distance to the ocean, having coffee with mates, finding eclectic and rare vinyl records, sinking my teeth into projects, learning new music on the guitar and spending more time hanging out with my wife. These might sound like the simple pleasures, reserved for weekends or days off, but for me, this is what I live for.

I have no doubt the things that bring me a sense of success will continue to evolve and change, but for now, it feels like a version of success which means more to me than any I'd achieved in the corporate world. I'd happily give back all the awards and trophies for that one moment when a client turned to me and said, "This is incredible Chris, what you've done here has transformed the way we look at everything." One fades and the other stays with you. The success I experience now, I want to continue to redefine, explore and grow to include more of what is possible within the life I already have.

One of the most rewarding realisations is to understand how the achievement of success does not require impossibilities like being a billionaire, having millions of followers or solving the world's problems. The relentless pursuit for 'more' and 'better/newer/brighter' things that our culture promotes, hides the true reality - all we need to be happy is to achieve a state of 'enough'. Not everyone can reach the position at the top, yet a real honest sense of success and happiness can still be achieved. To be really good at what you do, doesn't mean you have to be better than everyone else, it just means you have to be good 'enough' for yourself.

This is the real definition of success. It is the ability to know what is enough for you. Success can be achieved by looking at the world in a different way and seeing it is up to you to decide what success even looks like in the first place.

# CHAPTER TWENTY
*Term 2: Design a career*

My parents were of the generation that believed in 'job-for-life' careers. Like many in the Baby-boomer era, following their school years, they picked a job and stuck with it until they retired. I grew up thinking this was the way careers worked. But unlike my parents, computers, the internet and mobile technology came along early in my working life. Like many other people in their early twenties who experienced the dramatic change in work within a mere one-two years, I was not only forced to change how I worked very quickly, but I also saw the effects of advances in technology on the careers of the people who couldn't keep up with a changing job market.

The same principles surprisingly still apply today, but in a very different way. We live in a world where many jobs rely on the votes of corporate shareholders, reduced body counts and ever-increasing work expectations. Work requirements are no longer just about keeping up with changes in technology affecting the skills we need to do our jobs. There continues to be significant changes and uncertainty across many industries now calling for people to not just be a cog in the machine.

So, what does a career realistically look like these days? The typical perception has changed substantially over the last decade, due to technology, globalisation and connect-ability. We've become more time-poor than ever, productivity now dominates our lives, and 'career' takes on a whole new meaning.

When it comes down to it, the differences between working for someone else and working for yourself are few. Yet these differences can impact significantly on the wellbeing of many people.

Working in a traditional job can mean long commutes, strict office hours, no choice over who you work with (and therefore office politics), but it also comes with the benefits of regular pay cheques and often the ability to turn off all responsibility when you power down at the end of the week. Whereas working for yourself can mean late nights and weekends on your computer, little separation between life and work, instability of clients and projects, volatility of inconsistent paydays, yet a sense of ultimate freedom, the reward of self-discipline and devotion to earning an income.

The opportunity to experience freedom and fulfilment is there in both career paths, but often it's the freedom of choice available to a person when working independently, which makes it the natural choice for many.

Let me be clear, I still believe corporate jobs are a significant part of the career landscape. I have friends, relatives and ex-colleagues who happily thrive in their fields as senior managers, executives and directors. But they clearly have a tolerance for it. I sometimes wonder if I could've found an ounce of tolerance, if I'd persevered or been more patient. But I decided it was more productive for me to challenge what it all meant and whether it was what I really wanted.

In the end, I was led by my purest instinct - my heart, and not by anything else.

It's better to be aware of what kind of career you're suited to sooner, rather than later. We should question whether the career we think we need will give us the life we know in our heart-of-hearts we undoubtedly want. We should find out what it is like to work in the industry that sparks our interest, to know how things honestly function on a day-to-day basis, in the good times and bad. If we follow a career direction knowing the kinds of challenges confronting us, we can better understand whether we have the passion, the fire and the devotion to find fulfilment even when things get tough.

I don't believe we should ever underestimate the value of diverse experience in our chosen industry. If I hadn't gone through all I'd gone through over twenty years of employment, if I didn't discover the way things had always been done, then I wouldn't have had the insider knowledge to create Taco Stand. Understanding how an industry works from all perspectives can give you the insight to challenge how it operates and see the gaps that can be filled with your skills, outside of and complimentary to a traditional job description.

The traditional work environment teaches us, or more accurately - requires us, to mould ourselves to fit into the jobs available. We have to change ourselves, our career goals, and sometimes our most productive method of working to tick all the boxes of the job description we're expected to fill. But with self-employment and freelance work, we can focus on building our own position descriptions, dictated by market demands and opportunities. The beauty of this is when we apply independence to traditional structured thinking, our specific skill-set can become our 'art'. By looking at career or work as 'art', it puts an emphasis on finding a way to creatively apply our skills to our desired industry.

Art is driven by your heart's desires, it's what you choose to put on display for the world to see. Like anything that comes from your heart it can't be edited down or compromised, otherwise it's incomplete, it's not you. The thing about art is, it's difficult to hide when you find it. It puts you at your most vulnerable and not everyone is going to get it. But that's okay. Art comes from your unique place. From all of your experiences, your passions, desires and inspirations. It's how you can leave your mark and how you can make a difference.

In the professional sphere of business, there is a lingering belief that things need to be done in a certain way. Business practises tend to follow the theories of supply and demand, with the pursuit of growth and higher profits the defining method of achieving business sustainability. But there is no 'enough' in this space and these approaches can treat employees as a liability, an expense on the balance sheet, in the pursuit of more.

As individuals, with career and personal aspirations, a smarter choice is to take a different approach to our long-term career prospects in the professional sphere. If we take an artist's view of our careers, we can instead apply our skills and knowledge in creative ways to achieve results. This gives us an opportunity to build something more than profits before people.

To take an artist's view requires the ability to look at the world, and your career, differently. To do this, I took my previous job roles and looked separately at each of the tasks I was required to do. Every task involves a suite of skills or knowledge, and when we detail those skills and knowledge it's easy to see how they can also be applied in other ways. What this requires is looking back at the past to understand what you are capable of, so you can then look forward at all the options, alternatives and potential adventures, which may simply require a new way of working.

For me, this meant applying specific skills and knowledge to fill a gap in a very specific way. I maximised all opportunities with the things I was very good at, while minimising completely the need to use my weaknesses. This approach will never fit into a traditional job description, but it was perfect to create a niche business that gives me the ability to be selective and creative. And this business fits into the life I want to live.

Designing your own career may begin with a traditional job, company or work experience you have, but has the flexibility to change and grow as you do. There are companies offering this to employees, but often it is freelance roles that are able to be tailored to a specific skill-set. Part of this is applying your talents to the right business and clients, who not only need your skills, but who get you and what you are trying to achieve.

# CHAPTER TWENTY-ONE
*Term 3: Live life*

We only get one shot at life.

I know, this sounds like some stupid cliché, or one of a billion motivational-posts passing your screen every day. But it's true. And it's one of the hardest concepts of life to really grasp the importance of.

I think it's difficult to understand what this means because it doesn't just refer to the fact that life is short and we might never get to realise some of the dreams we have, or that time with people we love is precious. What it is really telling us is that we only get to live each day, each week, each month and each year - once. Yet, we fill our seconds, minutes and hours with the things we 'should-do', or 'have-to-do', because we think 'some-day' will actually come. In reality the only things we have-to-do are the things keeping ourselves and our loved ones alive, like food on the table, clothes on our backs and a roof over our heads.

This became scarily real for me during the research trip my wife and I had to Bali before moving there. I was out surfing on my favourite reef break, when the boat captain, a local Balinese man who'd become a friend over the years, came to collect me with his young daughter, a nervous passenger in the small fishing boat. Shortly after climbing onboard, the motor died, and we began to drift into the wave's impact zone. We tried desperately to get it started, to no avail. On our last attempt we pulled the cord completely off its spool. We had limited options at this point, and in a moment that will forever haunt my days, a set wave towered over the boat before violently throwing it upside-down.

My split-second decision to throw my surfboard and leap as the wave turned us mid-air meant I was able to recover quickly, surfacing to see only the bottom of the boat above water as a second wave crashed down on top of it. Time stopped as I dove back under to desperately find my friend and his young daughter, silently praying they too had managed to find their way clear of the boat.

Fear entered my heart as I saw the young girl struggling and her father not far away. I pulled her up to the surface and onto my surfboard and went back for my friend, who came up in the seconds between dives. All three of us clung to my board, shaking from the adrenalin as we waved down a passing fisherman to help us get back to shore.

The event that passed between my friend and I changed how I viewed the fragility of life and the brutality of the ocean. It brought us closer as we shared an instant depth of connection, which binds people together in a life-threatening accident.

However, it wasn't just this accident that made me see I only had one shot at life. And it wasn't the two other times I escaped serious harm on this particular holiday due to freak waves and busted boards. It was actually in the first week we arrived back in Bali, ready to start our new adventure. I raced down to see my friend again, hopefully to convince him to come out for a wave. But when I got down to his warung, I was greeted by one of his workers, who told me in the only way he knew how, "Ketut no longer here. He gone." Just weeks before we arrived at our new home, only two months since I'd seen him last, my friend had died from heart failure due to unknown causes.

I'll be the first to admit, I don't handle devastating news well. I didn't quite know how to react or what to say to his wife and daughters when I saw them again. In a culture where family are the foundation of everything, the loss of a loved one must be irreconcilable. It also made me see that even if a person is strong and capable, it doesn't mean they are 'peril resistant'.

Ketut's death was a wakeup call like never before. It made me see clearly how our decision to move to Bali wasn't just an experiment in living away from Australia, it was an opportunity to live life the way we really wanted to. It affirmed our decision to not be influenced by all the 'should-do's' and 'have-to-do's' which for years had compelled us to stay in the same place, pursuing the same dreams as everyone else.

It would have been easy to conform to the lives of the people around us and to follow the path friends and family had taken. But for some people, like me, I didn't want to conform.

When we started to question the way things had always been done, we could see that we were in fact the only one responsible for making different choices. And living and working away from Western culture has helped make any inclination toward conformity a lot easier to question.

It often felt risky to challenge the choices everyone else was making. There was the risk of upsetting people we had no intention of hurting and there was the risk of getting it wrong and making mistakes. But until a person tries doing things differently, it's not really possible to know what the biggest risk is. Actually, I don't even think this is true, because the biggest risk is, we never find out just how great life can be.

I didn't want to wait until I was retirement age to move to a tropical island and surf in idyllic surf conditions every day. I wanted to do it while I was still young enough to make the most out of life. Many people still think, "well it is just not possible for me to choose what I want for my life", but in reality, I meet people every day, other expats, long-term travellers, young, old, married and with children of all ages who are living a life similar to mine. There is nothing special or particularly different about any of us except for the fact we wanted to live life in a manner that challenged what we'd done before.

I think it's a fair question for us to ask, what kind of life do you want to live? What do you want to be doing every day? Is it what you are doing now?

# PART FOUR
# FROTH & HUSTLE

*The Froth & Hustle Philosophy*

This is Froth & Hustle.

Based on the psychological and spiritual skills I gained through surfing, it was this personal philosophy that completely transformed my life. By applying Froth & Hustle to challenges faced every day, I built the career and lifestyle I never believed I could have. And in the process, it forever altered the way I viewed the world and my place in it.

Froth & Hustle follows three key principles that form the surfer's mindset. They impact both personal and professional life, in and out of the water, from communicating better to managing significant stress, and even improving the way business is done. Most importantly, this surfer's mindset facilitates the creation and realisation of 'art' - the thing each of us is most able and most qualified to give back to the world around us.

Before I learned to surf, the only escape I enjoyed was in playing sport, listening to and writing music, and going away on holidays. These outlets became a necessity for releasing adulthood pressure. I spent a great portion of my career wound up tighter than a two-dollar watch. I chose to deal with this all-consuming stress as most of us might, by focusing on what to do and never what to think. Then surfing entered my life.

Everything changed when surfing became a regular part of my week. It didn't happen instantly, but I could feel the potential from my very first wave. In the beginning, surfing was an effective way to liberate myself from the daily grind. But it provided me with so much more. I gained the ability to relax and calm my mind, one of the most life-altering things I ever learned. It infected every single thing I did, how I saw the world and how I functioned in it, health, relationships, work and happiness.

Through surfing I found a whole new level of relaxation, thanks to an all-consuming combination of focus and presence. I can be sitting out in the ocean, immersed in thoughts, until the moment my wave arrives. This is when I steer my mind to one thing and one thing only. Everything else disappears. My entire being is focused only on surfing.

When I'm at my most relaxed I glide into waves with perfect momentum. My transitions feel smoother, I feel more fluid, more natural, as though my board becomes an extension of my body. This is what absolute presence feels like to me. Not only do I seem to get more waves, I seem to attract more of the right kind of waves. When I'm in this state all my senses are heightened, yet my mind remains calm.

Being completely relaxed holds many benefits beyond just calming nerves, stress, anger or anxiety. It offers a complete state of awareness that opens new possibilities for understanding the importance of presence and detachment. This state triggers a deeper, more auto-intuitive response to the world around you. When we relax in the surf, we are open to all the signals, we become more adaptable. And in business this is the place we uncover opportunities and make smarter decisions. We tend not to force our opinions and ideas but rather cultivate them more organically.

Learning to relax dramatically changed not only my surfing, but all aspects of my work at Taco Stand. Now, the ability to relax is the foundation of my personal philosophy. From the laws of connection, to the state of flow and a willingness to let go, knowing how to relax underlies everything. Together these form a powerful mindset, the surfer's mindset - balanced, rational and open. It's a refined understanding of the most simplistic of theories - that what is, simply is.

## CHAPTER TWENTY-TWO
*Connect*

When I first learned to surf, I thought it would be like any new sport, taking just time and practise to master the correct techniques. My progression was painfully slow and incredibly frustrating, and at times, like many new surfers, I struggled to understand what I was doing wrong. But over the many years that I persevered and the many hours I spent in the water, sometimes surfing, sometimes just enjoying being out there, I became aware of a deeper sense of connection to the ocean that had developed alongside my passion for the sport. This was when everything started to change. This was my awakening.

Somehow, I'd completely overlooked an essential part of surfing.

As the connection became increasingly apparent, I began to approach the practise with a whole new way of being. Instead of applying only surfing techniques, I was now working in synergy with my environment. I was aware of my physical actions, but now I was using a felt-sense of motion to read the ocean's energy.

The difference to both my enjoyment and progression was

remarkable.

Conscious of an almost spiritual connection, I could now interpret even tiny changes in the ocean's movement. What was once a confusing washing machine, throwing up random peaks and constant struggles, suddenly became a fluid pattern that offered a playing surface of opportunities. I became alive to nature's power, gently persuading me to move with its rhythms. And when I allowed the wave to lead, my body adjusted through a natural process of interpretation. The ocean began to teach me how to surf.

This new, complex sensation compelled me to seek this energetic connection with the water again and again, to try to understand it better, to get it to work with me and for me.

Surfing was no longer just a sport. It became the metaphysical challenge I needed to 'plug me into life' every day.

In the ocean, I'm far removed from all distractions, life takes on a different focus and everyday pressures melt away into the distance. Schedules and deadlines seem to pause as energy filters into being exactly where I am. Worrying about the past or sweating the future is pointless when there are waves to catch.

When I struggle to connect to what I am doing, I'm usually following agendas, chasing low-priority desires, or trying to fill time - essentially, I've lost all awareness of what I should be focused on.

In many ways, to connect we must completely disconnect from what we call the 'real world', we need to disconnect from time, our thoughts and things in the periphery. When I disconnect in this way, I gain a healthier, more balanced, distanced perspective of life. In this process it's possible to dissolve many of the emotional and reactionary thoughts that otherwise influence my decision-making. Additionally, I've found my mind is filled with fresh ideas, simply by clearing out all of the unnecessary distractions. This is when the flood gates open. I'm able to resolve my most frustrating issues and make clearer decisions.

It's here that connecting can transform how we relate to the world around us.

The days when I'm surfing at my best, are coincidently the days I feel the most connected to the ocean, like a heightened awareness of its tempo and timing. It is something that permeates every cell of my body - a feeling I 'feel' beyond explanation.

Surfers often talk about the thrills of surfing, their adventures and their conquests, but I've spoken with only few who actively explore their deeper connection to the sea. Perhaps for many it's a personal relationship that doesn't require acknowledgement. But for me this relationship is grounding, it gets me out of my head and into reality. The importance of this has been made abundantly clear to me every time an injury has kept me away from the waves. The longer my absence, the more desperate I become to reconnect.

When surfing, we connect to something far greater than our self. This connection is a privilege, it can change the way we think and teach us valuable lessons. With it comes numerous physical and psychological benefits, which act as the gateway to awareness and understanding of the world.

The surfer's ability to connect isn't exclusive to their relationship to the surf, this connection can be explored on a personal level. Although harnessed as a tool to help improve surfing, the ability to connect also deepens experience in other parts of life, with people, our surroundings and our work.

A surfer stands before the ocean, no agenda, no routine, just technical ability and instinct. We learn to play what's in front of us, at any specific moment. A surfer can make a bad wave good, and sometimes, luck hands us the dream barrel, but over time we develop the necessary skills and technique, to balance bodily power with mental focus. But this can only take place with an unwavering connection to and acceptance of what the ocean offers.

A surfer needs to be focused to see the wave opportunities and take them. And business is exactly same. Having the tools or techniques is simply not enough. I need to have the same focus, flexibility and adaptiveness in business that I possess in the ocean, to connect with clients on a level that has an impact. Without connection, there's no true progress, no dream ride, just frustration.

It might be possible to get potential clients to meet with you or take your call, but this doesn't mean you have any lasting relationship. Initiating communication is just the first step and a true connection must be allowed to evolve over time. A business relationship can never be forced, owned or claimed, they continue to evolve as the environment they are in ebbs and flows. To be effective, we must evolve with it and keep working to maintain connections within changing business environments.

True connections are based on authenticity. They may begin with a desire to feel in sync with something, but every true connection hinges on the capacity for honesty and transparency. This is why surfers are in a unique position to discover the importance of connection. A surfer can only be authentic with the waves.

There's nowhere to hide in the ocean, it's as brutally honest as it is unpredictable. All layers of bravado are stripped back, when a surfer faces off with the power of nature.

The human vulnerability that is exposed in the relationship between surfer and ocean, is often the very same thing that prevents people from connecting authentically on dry-land. Many would believe that holding the world at-arms-length provides a necessary barrier to the perceived dangers of authentic connection. But these dangers are based solely on comfort zones and 'professional correctness'. However, behind every professional and every brand is a real person.

People always feel and respond to an authentic connection, it's what they remember most. Authenticity builds trust and confidence; it shows the other party that you are willing to put everything else aside to genuinely connect.

The strength of our relationships aren't measured by a handshake and promise of goodwill. They are formed over time through challenges and difficulties. Nothing is ever as it seems on the surface of a connection. Often, it's what we can't see but what we feel that delivers both the greatest opportunity and the highest risk. It's not just about gaining a logical understanding of each other; it is about tuning-in at a deeper level and seeing the world through their eyes.

In the same way a surfer must connect mindfully with the ocean, an ability to focus energies into the person or task in front of you, connects you on an authentic level. If a surfer were to go out in big surf without mental focus and connection, they would be risking their life. It is not too dissimilar in a meeting or professional event; in fact, it is not too dissimilar to being with someone you care about.

I've sat in meetings, lunches and dinners with colleagues and clients, when the person who could benefit most from the interaction, clearly isn't there. This is a huge barrier to creating an authentic relationship with someone. Any connection over an extended period of time will be tested, this applies to one-on-one, business-to-business and brand-to-consumer relationships. So, if you're going show up, you better be there and not just in a physical sense. The person you are connecting with deserves your absolute attention and nothing less, you need to put 'all of yourself' in the room.

Viewing customer relationships from a holistic perspective has a lot to do with how successfully a brand or a business person understands the environment they operate in. Doing the work to connect authentically and regularly, enables business and customer relationships to develop into a life form of their own, evolving with each other and for each other, with both parties benefiting from the connection. If you can master this part of long-term connection and relationship successfully, you are well on your way to creating something of real substance.

# CHAPTER TWENTY-THREE
## *Flow*

I had already been surfing for several years before I noticed how my deepening connection to the ocean led me to what I can only describe as a state of flow. Self-taught, I was reasonably content with the surf-buzz I had experienced to date, but my inability to progress was frustrating at times and for a while I couldn't see past it. Again, I thought I was doing something wrong, but it had nothing to do with my technique. If anything, I was trying too hard to control what my body was doing, when I really just needed to relax and open up.

My break-through came shortly after I discovered my personal connection to the ocean. The strength of this metaphysical connection put me in the right frame of body and mind to effortlessly achieve a state of flow. This process of connection born into flow, spawned a new sense of personal rhythm. It became an organic motion that merged human energy with the water's power.

When I first began to experience a state of flow, time seemed to slow down. I had more space to interpret and feel what lay ahead and my understanding of the ocean environment suddenly felt natural. As every part of my body, mind and surfboard began to feel in sync with the wave, I developed trust in my own ability to glide with the ocean. I was able to accept the unknown before me and sharpen my vision to know the next move to make.

I found that flow has no formula, just feeling, harmony and rhythm. But above all other mechanics, flow feeds and stimulates opportunity. If we get into the right mindset to connect, flow becomes the vision, the expression and the launching pad for development and real growth.

The state of flow might unfold from focus and connection with the ocean; however, it is contingent on a surfer's capacity to come to terms with the unpredictability of nature's whim. Surfers have little choice but to concede to the randomness that is forced on us. But this is not an admission of defeat, it is the avenue to flow, where the unpredictability can be harnessed to identify new opportunities.

Many people fear the unpredictability and randomness of life. Companies spend millions to control outcomes and people invest endless energy trying to minimise random factors, maintain comfort zones and limit the need to face the unknown. But by trying to uphold a predictable and repetitive life, we limit both our experiences and ourselves, resulting in an atrophy of both physical and mental aptitude.

The beauty of life's randomness is it enables new discoveries, innovation, expansion of knowledge and improvements in the way we do things. It is the antidote to the patterns that create predictable states. Randomness makes us feel inspired and alive. And embracing it feeds our willingness to experience new things.

Whether it's an uncontrollable mess or super-glassy perfection, a surfer's first instinct is to look for ways to harness the ocean's energy and make the most of what's there. Whatever is being served up, we deal with it.

When sneaky set-waves come bearing down on a person in the ocean, it would be fruitless to ask, "why is this happening to me?". A set-wave's existence has very little to do with the person under its shadow. It's not a personal attack, it's just the way the ocean works, it's simply the way it is.

Accepting that randomness is a natural part of life encourages a person to relinquish the need to control their environment. It activates an important human function that tests and develops our response to the unexpected, building the capacity for three things: trust in our instincts, a greater understanding of the world around us and the ability to adapt to any circumstance. This strengthens our resilience when facing uncertainty or failure.

It is up to the surfer to work out how to make the most of random wave behaviour. Good or bad, in the surf we must act on instinct and in reaction to the things we can't control. It's impossible to force what we want onto the ocean; a surfer can only study the immediate environment and quickly adapt to achieve a desired outcome from the options in front of us.

Even though accepting the randomness of the ocean is essential to a surfer, it's also an extremely healthy perspective to apply on land. In my case, realising there was little I could control in my professional life made me aware of the opportunity I had to follow an alternative path, to do something different and unpredictable in my own way.

There's a great deal to learn from the approach surfers take when confronted with random changing conditions and uncertainty. Randomness in our everyday lives offers the possibility to be freed from comfort zones or self-imposed limitations that keep us stuck.

Comfort zones might have emotional benefits, but often they are the very thing holding a person back from experiencing growth and positive change. Whenever I've faced and accepted the challenge to push out of my comfort zones it has taught me to trust in my abilities, both in the ocean and in business. But I had to put myself into the challenging situation first and then go with the flow of what came of it.

I learned that nothing comes from staying where you are or waiting for something to happen within existing limitations. But being open to random conditions can take you on an unexpected journey to somewhere even better.

One of the greatest misconceptions of the term 'go with the flow' is that it requires you to not care about the outcomes of your life and just accept what the world has in store for you. Often attributed to being part of a surfer's mentality, the idea of 'going with the flow' is in fact quite the opposite of the lazy, careless attitude commonly referred to.

Flow isn't about giving up or allowing the world dictate to us. Instead, flow enables you to accept reality but take action on the changing conditions and opportunities around you. It is controlling what you can, within the flow of where you are.

When random changing events occur, immediate reactions tend to be in resistance or protest to what is happening. However, if an individual adopts a state of flow when faced with this uncertainty, the focus shifts from what went wrong to what can be made right.

Random and changing situations don't necessarily require contingency plans to survive them, but they do require trust in yourself to make the most effective choices. Trusting in instincts gives a person the confidence to think on their feet, but these instincts can only be developed through years of putting yourself out there.

A surfer knows you can't just paddle out and expect to catch your first wave. Every surfer has to understand the fundamentals of surfing and have a process to follow in the beginning. It is the experience gained through process that helps the surfer develop instinct, enabling the ease into flow.

The state of flow feels natural and is the complete opposite of self-consciousness. It's when a person doesn't need to stop and ask if what they are doing is right. It's when instinct takes over the reins to facilitate momentum. There's no stopping to edit out the ugly bits, just a creative momentum that makes the most of opportunities present.

Without doubt, being in a state of flow is the happiest I have ever been. There's a certain indescribable magic that happens when everything feels 'just right'. On these days my mind is sharper, my body more nimble, this is when something clicks, and I just know today is going to be a good day. It doesn't happen every time I surf, but this makes it more special when everything does line up and I feel at one with the world.

I am convinced, the state of flow is the most natural platform from which to expand creativity and talent. It is where hard skills progress from learning to creative development and expression. The progression comes from taking action, from getting your hands dirty, from trying new things and being prepared to not be good at something or even to fail. However, the secret we unlock within the state of flow is trust in our abilities, our movement and our growth, no matter how slow.

The state of flow is where we make the most substantial improvements to ourselves and the work we produce. I do my finest work when I'm in flow and it is imperative for my art. For this reason, the principals of flow are largely responsible for the very existence of Taco Stand. It's what sets me apart, and without these fundamental differences my work would be no different to anyone else's.

In flow, a person can work from an acute awareness and reaction to changing circumstances, relying heavily on flexibility and adaptiveness to the environment they're operating in. It's where a person's best expression, individuality and creativity comes from. It's not bedded in logical analysis; it's done in real time using the random elements available in the moment.

In surfing, flow is essential, it links turns, supplies momentum, provides balance and is at the core of power and progression. Flow provides the opportunity to find and inject personality and style into the physical actions, the fun part of feeling at one with the world around you. Flow helps you discover your signature and your art.

As a surfer glides across the wave, there's countless physical and mental factors at play. Physically, the technical ability to balance power and movement determines direction and speed. Every muscle finds a purpose - to move in sync. But mentally, surfers are steered by their ability to read the changing surface and be guided by instinct, agility and reflexes. It takes a cohesion of body and mind, of hard and soft skills, to enter a state of flow and find the opening to express art.

This same combination of hard and soft skills, of utilising knowledge and experience to stay flexible and creative within a changing environment, is the foundation of successful companies and brands. Every market has its own requirements, which brands build their mechanics and processes on. These mechanics, such as design, technology, marketing, finance and distribution models are just a small part of the brand equation, however. And while balancing the formula of these mechanics for a specific market may increase the brand's opportunity for placement, they must continue to grow, change and flow with the market and consumer environment they are in.

Long-term success of a brand is not based on a solid structure and platform, it is based on flexible mechanics that allow movement in line with consumer and market changes. This creates fluidity in the structures of a brand, and the ability to be creative when maximising opportunities.

True opportunities are almost always found below the surface. It goes well beyond building products at attractive price points, every brand needs to go deeper to build long-term success. To create something of substance, a business needs to stretch out beyond standard mechanics and formulas. Success relies heavily on an ability to read opportunities, develop momentum and creativity through a state of flow.

As per connection, the state of flow can't be forced it has no handles and no end point, it's a constant motion to improve and develop, organically and authentically. As product lifecycles shorten, as technology advances to replace itself, as margins are squeezed to death by the changing consumer environment, everyone needs to evolve and maintain their momentum, or they inevitably risk irrelevance. It takes more than ability, capacity, or desire to succeed, it takes flexibility and the honest awareness of what you need to change.

It takes physical and mental commitment to change with the world around you. And even the most connected of surfers, people or brands can lose momentum if they resist it. Ability and desire are critical, but useless without the flexibility that enables us to take action on change.

The greatest opportunities exist when you are completely connected to your environment and you adopt a state of flow that moves with it. Flow turns change into opportunity and resistance into creativity.

## CHAPTER TWENTY-FOUR
*Let Go*

In primary school, I regularly launched my skinny little body and BMX off dirt ramps with my mates at the local playground. Evil Knievel was my hero and I fancied myself as a potential future daredevil.

I loved the feeling of flying through the air, going higher and further. After each landing, we'd increase the stakes by building the ramp bigger and steeper, launching ourselves into the sky, flailing around until our wheels landed with a thud and we'd know we survived. We did this over and over again until one of us stacked it and we'd scamper home to have our wounds tended to. But all throughout the school holidays, we'd return day after day to challenge ourselves once again.

Despite the bruises and multiple grazes we suffered, nothing compared to the feeling we earned in constantly surprising ourselves by pushing the limits of our fear. The thrill of our rubber tires letting go of solid ground, was the moment of illumination. We just had to know what we were capable of.

Testing physical boundaries as a kid was a normal part of growing up, we've all done it in some shape or form. But as we get older, many of life's opportunities to test ourselves are prevented by the battle that takes place in our minds.

Whether it is testing our capacity for change, our skills to put forward innovative projects, or our desire to try something new, many of the biggest risks we have to take begin with a stand-off between comfort zones and possibility. The willingness to let go of comfort and control is a difficult thing to commit to and can feel alien in our otherwise predictable and secure environments.

Our modern lifestyles are largely based on zero-risk tolerance, nurtured by a need for comfort and safety. Our decisions on where to travel, what car to buy, the safest area to live, who to hire, what food to eat, are all based on what we are comfortable with and the decisions we have made before.

All true sense of adventure has been stripped away by a culture of data, reviews and recommendations, our predominant method of exploration exercised in the comfort of our homes, through the safety of our screens. We're quick to trade personal thoughts and curiosity for the perceived safety of mass opinion. But this convenience and comfort, starves our natural instinct to explore and suffocates our independent critical thought. Perhaps the only way to discover a spirit for exploration is to replace our predictable habits with random actions. Or maybe we need to simply unplug from technology and plug into the world around us.

Although most people already understand what it means to let go, I think it's possible very few of us do it when we actually need to. Many people continue to fear the unknown, demonstrated by the homogeneity of how we 'do' Western society. Opting for the well-worn path of predictability and the belief that 'this is the way we have always done things', productive and positive change is slow, laboured and resisted on many levels.

It's only when we try to move in a different direction, we can realise just how restricted, planned and automatic our thinking has become. For me, my search for the sense of letting go may have started with dare-devilling on a BMX, but it eluded me until I discovered it again in surfing.

Surfing has always acted as a salvation from the structures keeping me stuck and resistant. Every time I surf it freshens my mind, negating any 'automation' I might have collected on land. The surfing lifestyle has become an adventure in experimentation, one full of surprises, failures, lessons and with the right mindset, has led me to the greatest break-throughs.

In the ocean, a surfer has to let go of all expectations and simply act on the conditions within a moment. It's just the surfer and wave, connected, in flow and ready to experience a precise moment of mental release. It's in this moment a person can feel the positive impact that letting go has on breaking through their own limitations. In the surf, it's the perfect setting to explore what it means to discover our true ability to leap.

In surfing, a person needs to balance both control and letting go in perfect harmony. It begins with knowing how to control the mind to connect with the ocean environment, trusting in instincts to ease into an energetic flow. And it ends with letting go of all expectations so that the surfer can truly breakthrough to the next level and be present within the moment. Letting go is what facilitates real progression on the waves.

Development as a surfer comes from a place of not knowing what's going to happen next, by putting yourself in otherwise uncomfortable situations. But most people can't get there unless they let go of the fear that prevents them from even trying in the first place.

Letting go is really the capacity to open up the mind to new potentialities. It is releasing our hopes for the way things 'should' turn out, so we can maximise possibilities within the way things actually turn out. It's staying in control of your own mental environment, so you don't feel the need to have total control of the physical. If we're rigid, static or trying to stay in control, we simply can't progress any further than the straight line we are already on. It inhibits our ability to be free for new experiences.

We've all had those moments when we take a leap of faith and test our physical or mental abilities. But like any risk, in these moments we expose ourselves to all possibilities within a situation, both good and bad. However, most people are typically occupied by one possibility. The possibility of failure.

The fear of failure is what makes most people want to control outcomes, it is what makes us want to go in a straight line. But when we let go of the need to avoid failure, we have the opportunity to experience every other possibility, to discover what we are actually capable of. Professionally and personally, if we don't let go, we can't discover the delights and genuine excitement of breaking through.

Break-throughs in my professional life have led to thumping big orders that strained production, and in the ocean, breaking through meant surfing in conditions I didn't realise I could and surprising myself with untested ability. These are the kind of experiences that make your heart race with genuine excitement. These are the moments that I feel truly alive.

With no definitive expectation of outcomes, we are motivated to put our best efforts forward and let go. After all, once all of the hard work has been done, what's left to hang on to? Endless perfecting and practise are wasted if we don't allow ourselves to reach the moment when we let go of what we are trying to achieve, to get feedback from the world around us. There is no point in paddling out, unless we are prepared to commit, let go of our desired outcomes and just trust in our skill and connection with the ocean. We can't possibly know what is going to happen on this wave or in any aspect of our life, until we let go.

If we edit-down our commitment or efforts, to sway on the side of safety, it is almost certain we will face problems. Over analysis of a situation, can generate a 'fake instinct', one causing an individual to pull back, to succumb to resistance, usually at a pivotal moment.

Finding the gusto to take the leap is not an easy one for most of us, but often the reasons we convince ourselves of to not take the leap, run deeper than those we rationalise in our heads. More often than not, at the root of all reasoning to not take a leap, is a web of logic woven by fear.

Despite popular belief, fear is not just 'false evidence appearing real'. Fear is as real as it can get to the person experiencing it, but this doesn't mean it's not conquerable. The thing is, fear belongs to the person holding it, and it is therefore totally in their power to do with it what they want. Most people who don't understand this blindly hold onto the fear, letting it grow bigger and more powerful over time. But for those who know better, the process of connecting with their environment and embracing the state of flow enables them to be so present with the world, they can just let go of the power the fear holds over them. The fear is still there, but they take the leap anyway.

This is actually the predominant reason why taking risks can be the most exhilarating moments in our life. Doing the things that cause us the most fear, in spite of the very fears we have, helps us reach unchartered territories within our own consciousness. These moments show us what we are capable of physically and mentally, in business and in life.

Letting go can only happen when a person is rightfully able to trust in themselves and connect with the environment they are in. This is not just about courage or even confidence in yourself, it is the ability to win the battle in our own minds so we can function at our very best, even in challenging situations.

If we're driven by an intention to break-through, it stands to reason that we already know we're holding back and we're curious to test what we are actually capable of. Seeking to understand and push your abilities to the limit, helps you to continuously break-through and set new thresholds.

Sometimes things don't turn out as we'd planned, I've taken many risks and had many failures to attest to this but putting in anything less than everything you've got is not only a compromise of your best work, it's not a true reflection of yourself. Backing down from a challenge or an opportunity to grow will stay with you much longer than the sting of failure.

A person can have all the confidence in the world, but if they maintain an attachment to the outcomes, this confidence won't make a difference to how we feel when the pivotal moment comes or if things don't turn out as planned. Defeat only feels like defeat if you have a narrow idea of what an outcome should look like. If we let go of our expectations as we take the leap, then we are able to roll with whatever happens.

Through my own failures and moments of defeat, I developed the self-awareness to find my own process for letting go. If I find myself hesitating when making a risky decision, I ask myself honestly, "Am I operating out of fear or instinct?".

Going through the process of letting go of material possessions, past experiences and wrong choices was actually pretty easy in hindsight. What did challenge me, however, was removing my attachment to future expectations and fear of future failures. This stuff was deeply ingrained within my behaviour. It had shaped a significant portion of my psyche and influenced many of the critical decisions I was faced with.

It was confronting to recognise this, but when I realised I no longer wanted the life I had worked so bloody hard for, in that moment I had little choice but to accept it and let go. My significant professional break-throughs only came after this critical moment, and if not exclusively reliant upon, then certainly influenced by my ability to let go. Over time I've made the conscious choice to see attachment and expectations for what they are and to view risk and limitations in a whole new positive light.

Everybody seeks the "wow, I really did that" moment. But it's reserved for those who are willing to take the leap and accept the risks involved. If it doesn't work out, a person can learn from the failure, and often it's possible to see just how unjustified all the fear was in the first place. The only way to honestly know, is to take the chance. It's as simple as that.

Now, when I look back at my career I can see where I stayed safe, mainly to protect my lifestyle or trophy cabinet. There was always a justification. Negativity trumped any short-lived optimistic thoughts about wondrous possibilities of having my own business. I didn't want to lose the car and I didn't want to change my comfortable lifestyle. Little did I know, this comfort brought about a form of stress and anxiety that turned out to be the core reason I couldn't progress in the way I always wanted.

My earlier days surfing were much the same. Instead of being fluid and open, I was tight and rigid, not releasing anything through fear of looking like a kook. It wasn't until I let go of this need to control the outcomes, that I tapped into what was really possible. I learned quickly that anything designed to enable improvement or break-through needed one hundred percent commitment. And this means accepting that if you don't stick the landing it's going to hurt, and there's nothing you can do about it. All you can do is accept you didn't get it right this time and persist to learn to do it the right way.

Making mistakes became my biggest asset. I learned far more from my mistakes than all the experiences handed to me on a silver platter with little risk involved. By looking for the constant feedback I received both in the surf and from the people I worked with, I learned to trust in my abilities and find the smartest way forward. The more I did this, the more aware I became of the golden opportunities right in front of me.

Learning to let go was the final phase in the development of a surfer's mindset that helped me see what was truly important to invest my energy in. It enabled me to achieve a lifestyle that always seemed out of reach. And it allowed me to experience life with a depth greater than I knew was possible.

I don't ever want to be left wondering "what if I'd only…?". It is the unknown within the possibilities of life where you find THE greatest excitement of our existence.

*Conclusion*

Surfing is a beautiful art-form played out in nature, created through a focus on only the present. There is something surreal about bringing this to life in any given moment. But the true magic of surfing can only be recognised when we identify the very particular benefits surfing offers to every aspect of life.

Froth & Hustle is about applying the surfer's mindset to transform our lives, by searching for a different philosophy - one connecting us deeply to the world and giving us the freedom to seek opportunities unencumbered by fears.

*Acknowledgements*

Writing this book was harder than I could've imagined. So, I'll start by thanking my entire editing and publishing team of one - my incredible wife, Stacey Marie, without whom this book wouldn't exist. Thank you, not just for your expertise and guidance but for your love, unwavering support and immeasurable patience; for believing I had something to say, worthy of countless hours tearing apart long-hand dribble and piecing it delicately back together to create something I can be proud of - Thank You.

To my Mom and Dad, you've given me more than a son could ever ask for. I'm sure it wasn't easy being my parents, I truly appreciate how much you've done and sacrificed to provide me with everything I needed, including the freedom to be me - Thank You. To my sister Karen and brothers Gary and Steve for helping me find my place in the world. Although I never say it, I'm forever grateful to have been your little brother, you helped shape me and my personality, you encouraged me to pursue life-long passions and you supported me without question when I needed it most. Also to my chosen family, Guy and Amy, my Sydney brother and sister - thank you for the unplanned barbecues, last minute trailer-runs and precious basement space that made our move overseas possible; Nat for the quality hours spent in the water and on dry-land; and to Rob (Collaroy's most handsome man) for the morning smiles, coffee and wisdom.

Thank you to all my close mates and surf buddies with who I've shared the waves over the years; Tristan who got me started - what a gift to prize someone with; Zadro for the company, fake surf reports and epic weekend sessions; Ric for filling the chilly Sydney air with laughter; Mike for making the most beautiful boards known to man; and the entire Longy crew. And the surfers who have made Bali feel like home; to Jon-Jon for the insightful worldly discussions and observations; Kunchan 'Mr. Backhand Attack' for your constant smiles and encouragement; Tonz for bringing love to those early morning walkouts; Kombong for never looking back; Koming for always being on time; Hollywood for the inspiring hair styles; and my Japanese brother Bobby-Sun - Arigatou!

Thank you to the guys who taught me to take off my muddy boots before entering the house, the local gardeners who set me on a path that was unexpectedly fulfilling; to Dan, who grounded me in the garden and shoved that first rake into my hands; Tiz, for being a black-belt certified legend; Matt 'Chiko' for fat Fridays, relentless advice and being a great mate by helping me get started on my own; and to Steely and Ben who fed me work and propped me up when I needed it most.

I would also like to thank the work colleagues over the years, who either put up with me or kept me sane, especially those who became friends along the way; Rob 'Barney', who saved my bacon when I needed it most; to Ben, Tina and Grant for the massive support; to Matty for doing a superb job and your best to keep it light; to Jay, with whom I've shared many years of good times and mate-ship; and to Francis, for your partnership, support, trust and loyalty. And to those less lucky, tasked with the annoyance of keeping me on track; Jonathon who gave me my first break and inspired a profession in me; Wayne, for taking a punt on a Sydney boy and believing in me;

Graeme for the trust, patience and fun times we enjoyed; and to Don, thank you for your humour, inspiration and generosity with your time.

And lastly, to my extended friends and family, my sincere thank you for accepting me into your lives. You have all contributed in some way to Froth & Hustle.

*Author's Biography*

Growing up in a land-locked city, Chris Brown only started surfing in his late 20's. Already an accomplished professional, his obsession with the surf began just in time to save him from an existence that revolved solely around work. Now as Director of Taco Stand, an international sales consultancy business based out of Australia, when he's not helping brands improve, you can find him in the ocean chewing the fat with other like-minded souls about how great life is when they're riding waves.

While surfing contributed to managing the stress of a corporate job, it was Chris's drive to pursue a balanced life that enabled him to take everything he learnt in the corporate world and apply it in a different way to design the career of his dreams.

Between surfing and Chris's other passions, he has authored his first book, *Froth & Hustle*, a study into how life is enhanced by applying a surfer's mindset to life outside of the water.

www.tacostand.co

## Artist's Biography

Monez is a Balinese illustrator, influenced by the fables of his childhood. While he began drawing at a young age, by the end of high school, he was called to a future in his family's garment business. After a short career in the factory office, Monez opposed family tradition and pursued a Master of Art at The Indonesian Institute of the Arts. He chose the road his grandfather, a painter, had taken. Inspired by Balinese culture and the folk-tales that drove his obsession with monsters, Monez developed a style called "Fablelous", a modern interpretation of his cultural traditions.

Today Monez's work can be seen in many forms, from large-scale murals to characters in children's books, at exhibitions in Asia, Africa and the United States to collaborations with Apple, Disney and Starbucks, and as a featured artist on design apps Affinity Designer and Procreate to the apparel and stationery he sells under the brand MONSTERO.

www.monez.net

www.ingramcontent.com/pod-product-compliance
Lightning Source LLC
Chambersburg PA
CBHW032037290426
44110CB00012B/846